Phonics 5

for Young Catholics

by

Seton Staff

Seton Press
Front Royal, Virginia

Executive Editor: Dr. Mary Kay Clark
Editors: Seton Staff

Printed in the United States of America

Seton Press
1350 Progress Drive
Front Royal, VA 22630
Phone: (540) 636-9990

For more information, visit us on the Web at: www.setonpress.com
Contact us by e-mail at: info@setonpress.com

ISBN: 978-1-60704-054-5

Cover: *The Annunciation*, by Eustache Le Sueur

**Dedicated to the
Sacred Heart of Jesus**

Table of Contents

Introduction

Phonics for Young Catholics 5 was written to teach fifth grade level phonics and word study. This text workbook does not go over basic phonics which students would have learned in earlier grades, but does cover more advanced concepts.

Notice that the phonics includes sounds for K, CH, G, WH, SH, GN, EAR, ILD, and so on.

Digraphs and diphthongs are covered, such as AI and AY, EE and EI, AU and AW, OI and OY, OU and OW.

Prefixes and suffixes are learned, as well as roots, compound words, possessives, plurals, and contractions.

This text workbook was written for the Catholic home schooling family. Consequently, each lesson contains a good number of references to Catholic beliefs and Catholic cultural family life.

Lesson plans and tests are available for students enrolled in Seton Home Study School.

A good dictionary, such as the *Merriam-Webster's Intermediate Dictionary* sold by Seton, would be helpful for the student.

Lesson 1 - k Sounds

Rule: In a syllable or word, the letters **k**, **ck**, or **que** usually will stand for the **k** sound.

Letters	Word	Sound
k	keys	k
ck	black	k
que	clique	k

DIRECTIONS: Read the phrases below. Answer the questions and circle the letters that make the **k** sound.

a kindly king   a blackrobe's pack   a unique antique

1. What would you call a generous monarch? a kindly king
2. What would you call a Jesuit priest's bundle? a blackrobe's pack
3. What would you call the Holy Grail? a unique antique

DIRECTIONS: Words containing **k**, **ck**, or **que** are hidden in the puzzle below. Some go across, and others go up and down. Find the words in the puzzle and circle them. Then, list words in alphabetical order under each spelling below.

rock   marks   cassock   boutique   sick   tack   kitten

peck   clique   Quaker   mystique   keys   unique

```
X C R D K S I K L M O D
P L C R I V R E M L T B
Z I R L T W C Y N G U O
D Q P V T C A S I C K U
Q U A K E R S L L U H T
J E K P N G S O N N P I
P E C K T R O C K I R Q
Q V C L L A C K L Q N U
B O U M A R K S Z U U E
M Y S T I Q U E C E L Y
```

k words	**ck** words	**que** words
marks	Lack	boutique
Quaker	rock	mystique
kitten	Peck	clique
keys	Sick	unique
	cassock	

Lesson 2 - qu & kn Sounds

Rules: 1. In a word or syllable, the letters **qu** sound like **kw**.

2. When **k** comes before **n**, it is not sounded. The letters **kn** sound like **n**.

Letters	Words	Sound
qu	queen	kw
kn	know	n

DIRECTIONS: Use the words below to fill in the blanks. Circle the letters that make the sounds **kw** or **n**.

Queen knight question kneel Knock quest quick know

1. You should ______________ the True Faith.
2. Mary is the ______________ of Heaven.
3. The ______________ went on a ______________ for the Holy Grail.
4. Christ said, "______________ and it shall be opened unto you."
5. You must ______________ when the Blessed Sacrament is exposed.
6. Can you answer the ______________?
7. If you move fast, you are ______________.

DIRECTIONS: Find the words in the puzzle; circle them; write them below in the correct column.

knowledge
acquire
knee
quicksand
equivocate
inquisition
Quakers
question
knock

```
B E Q U I V O C A T E L
C R U G N Q L D L R B M
R S O P Q U A K E R S Z
Q W K M U I M N C A Q U
K N E E I G G O A L U S
N O R N S K R W C T I T
O C Y A I S U L Q N C X
C G L Z T N C E U U K P
K I O R I O B D I R S R
N G F K O D H G R S A A
J M S L N W N E E P N L
K N Q U E S T I O N D W
```

kn words

____

____

____

qu words

____

____

____

____

____

____

Lesson 3 - ch Sounds

Rule: The letters **ch** can sound like **ch** or **k**. On rare occasions, **ch** can sound like **sh**, such as in chandelier or Charlotte.

Letters	Words	Sounds
ch	choir	k
ch	church	ch
ch	chivalry	sh

DIRECTIONS: Use the words below to fill in the blanks. Circle the correct sound, **ch**, **sh**, or **k**, for the word.

bench	chenille	chateau	leech	character	Christmas
choir	chastity	chrism	lunch	chandelier	chaperones

1. The player sat on the ____________________. **k ch sh**
2. The Christendom College ____________________ sang Gregorian chant. **k ch sh**
3. Christ's birthday is ____________________ day. **k ch sh**
4. There were four adult ____________________ at the teen party. **k ch sh**
5. We discussed modesty and ____________________ in our religion class. **k ch sh**
6. The ____________________ is a type of parasite which sucks blood. **k ch sh**
7. The ____________________ is the French knight's castle. **k ch sh**
8. The bishop used ____________________, a blessed oil, for Confirmation. **k ch sh**
9. We say the Angelus at noon before ____________________. **k ch sh**
10. Her bedspread is made of pink ____________________. **k ch sh**
11. My brother played the main ____________________ in the play. **k ch sh**
12. Mom bought a beautiful cut-glass ____________________ for the dining room. **k ch sh**

Lesson 4 - c Sounds

Rule: The letter **c** usually sounds like **k** or **s**.

The letter **c** usually has a hard **k** sound when it comes before **a**, **o**, or **u**.

The letter **c** usually has a soft **s** sound when it comes before **e**, **i**, or **y**.

Letter	Words	Sounds
c	catacombs	k
c	incense	s

DIRECTIONS: Circle each word in the story that has a **c** that sounds like **k** or **s** *before a vowel*.

In 1492, Columbus discovered America. He brought the Catholic faith to the New World. He found that the Indians were crude and barbaric.

Many Indians were converted by the Catholic missionaries who came with Columbus. The Mass was offered in crowded huts until churches could be built. Other devotions, like Benediction with incense, processions, and novenas, came when the missionary chapels were built.

The celebration of the Mass was a joyous event. The Indians were concerned and impressed that Jesus Christ was crucified for them on a cross. They came long distances to attend Mass. They traveled down rivers by canoe. They gave the missionaries their most valuable crop, corn.

DIRECTIONS: List the circled words in the proper column below. If a word appears more than once, write it only once. One word goes in both columns.

c sounded as **s**

c sounded as **k**

Lesson 5 - g Sounds

Rule: The hard sound of **g** is found in **garden**. It comes before **a**, **o**, or **u**.

The soft sound of **g** is like a **j** sound, as in **gym**. It comes before **e**, **i**, or **y**.

Letter	Words	Sounds
g	game	g
g	angels	j

DIRECTIONS: Read each word. If you don't know it, please look it up in the dictionary. Write **g** on the line if the word has a hard **g** sound, **j** on the line if the word has a soft **g** sound.

angelic	______	Evangelists	______	God	______
congregation	______	gold	______	Goliath	______
goose	______	giant	______	Gospel	______
genuflect	______	ginger	______	homage	______
goal	______	marriage	______	Genesis	______
indulgence	______	theology	______	generous	______

DIRECTIONS: Fill in the missing words with a word from above.

1. The four ____________________ wrote the Gospels.
2. Priests study ____________________ in the seminary.
3. Our eternal ____________________ is to reach Heaven.
4. Catholics ____________________ before the Blessed Sacrament.
5. In the parable, the good employer was ____________________ to all his workers.
6. The ____________________ knelt at the consecration of the Mass.
7. ________________ is the first book of the Bible.
8. Mother uses spices, including __________________ , when she bakes pumpkin pie.
9. A plenary __________________ takes away the temporal punishment due for our sins.
10. ________________ is a sacrament our parents received.
11. Sally likes to hear the Bible story about David and the __________________.
12. Did you read the story about the ____________ that laid the ____________ egg?

Lesson 6 - g Sounds

DIRECTIONS: In the sentences below, circle each word that has a hard or soft **g** sound followed by a vowel. Then, write the circled words in the correct sound column.

1. The Vulgate is the Latin version of the Bible translated by St. Jerome.
2. A vigil is the day before a feast day.
3. The baby started to giggle at her brother.
4. St. Francis of Assisi was given the stigmata by God.
5. Sanctifying grace is a supernatural gift.
6. The Catholic religion gives us the fullness of Faith.
7. The Propagation of the Faith Association supports Catholic missions in poor lands.
8. There are six holy days of obligation in the United States.
9. One of the liturgical books is on Martyrology.
10. An indulgence is granted to wipe out temporal punishment for sin after the guilt has been forgiven.
11. Guardian angels protect and guide us all our lives.
12. At Lourdes, the Blessed Mother wore a white gown.
13. We genuflect on both knees when the Blessed Sacrament is exposed.
14. St. Thomas Aquinas has the title, "Angelic Doctor of the Church."

g sounding as **j**	**g** sounding as **g**	
______	______	______
______	______	______
______	______	______
______	______	______
______	______	______
______	______	______
______	______	______
______	______	

Lesson 7 - Review

DIRECTIONS: Read aloud the paragraph below. See if you pronounce the **k**, **ck**, **kn**, **ch**, **c**, and **g** correctly. Mother may ask you to spell some words orally.

St. John Bosco wrote a book about St. Dominic Savio, a young boy who lived a saintly life and whom he had taught in boarding school. Dominic was always looking for penances to do, and sometimes jeopardized his health. One morning, John Bosco found Dominic shivering in his bed because he refused to use a blanket.

"What is the meaning of this?" I asked. "Do you want to die of cold?"

"I won't die of cold," he answered. "Jesus had even less to cover Him in the manger and on the Cross."

Then it was that I absolutely forbade him to do any penance without first getting permission from his confessor. This order he obeyed, but sadly.

One day, I noticed he was looking worried.

"Father," he complained, "I really don't know what to do! Our Lord tells me that unless I do penance, I can't get to Heaven, but you won't let me do any! What are my chances for Heaven?"

"The penance Our Lord asks of you," I answered, "is obedience. Obey and you will be doing enough."

"But won't you please let me do some other penance?"

"Yes, I will let you do the penance of daily bearing up with injuries, suffering heat, cold, tiredness, wind, rain, and all the discomforts of weak health which God sends you."

"But I have to suffer these things anyway."

"Then offer it all to God, and it will become virtue, and bring you merit."

Lesson 8 - Review

DIRECTIONS: We study phonics so that we can learn to read good literature to bring us closer to Jesus. Please read another passage about St. Dominic Savio from the book by St. Don Bosco.

One day, some thoughtless youngster who did not belong to the [Catholic] school brought into the yard a magazine with some indecent pictures. A group of boys gathered about to look at those cartoons which would have brought a blush to a pagan. Dominic, too, ran up, thinking there was something funny to look at. But when he got close enough to see, he stopped short and, with a look of scorn on his face, he took the magazine and tore it into pieces. A hush settled over the crowd. The boys looked at each other.

"Heaven help us!" exclaimed Dominic. "God has given us our eyes to look at His beauties, and you use them to stare at this filth made by bad men to corrupt your souls. Have you forgotten everything you have been taught? Our Lord says we can commit sin with a single glance, and then you go ahead and gloat over this filth!"

"We were only laughing at the cartoons," one remarked in excuse.

"Sure, laugh now!" replied Dominic. "Laugh yourselves right into Hell! Do you think you will still be laughing when you land there?"

"But there's nothing so terribly wrong with these pictures," objected another lad.

"Worse for you!" was Dominic's answer. "If you can't see anything wrong in this filth, it's because your eyes are used to it, but that does not excuse you! It only makes you more guilty! Poor old Job! A holy, old man, stretched out on a bed of pain, and yet he made a pact with his eyes not to look at anything shameful!"

All were silent.

On another day, a lad became violently abusive. He called Dominic names and then punched and kicked him. Savio could have returned the beating because he was bigger and stronger. But such revenge was not his. Though his face burned with anger, Dominic controlled himself and only replied, "You have acted very badly. But I'll forget it! Only don't try it on anyone else!"

Lesson 9 - the f Sound

Rule: The letters **f**, **ff**, and **ph** sound like **f**.

Letters	Words	Sound
f	faith	f
ff	sufficient	f
ph	phone	f

DIRECTIONS: Read the sentences aloud. Circle the **f** sound letter or letters. Circle the answer to the questions about that word.

1. The pontiff was John Paul II.
   What is a pontiff?
   a preacher | a pope | a fisherman

2. He will make his Confirmation in May.
   What is Confirmation?
   a film | a feast | a sacrament

3. Christ called the Pharisees hypocrites.
   Who were the Pharisees?
   religious leaders | Americans | Frenchmen

4. Priests and nuns recite the Divine Office.
   What is the Divine Office?
   fish | phones | prayers

5. The Easter lilies on the altar are very fragrant.
   What does fragrant mean?
   ruffle | fireproof | sweet-smelling

6. Veronica's veil looks like a photo of Christ's face.
   What does photo mean?
   phrase | picture | phonics

7. The bishop gave the new priest his faculties.
   What does faculties mean?
   photo albums | physical education | authority to function

8. Women's suffrage was passed in the 1800s.
   What does suffrage mean?
   french fries | staff | right to vote

Lesson 10 - the *f* Sound

DIRECTIONS: Circle the letter or letters that make the **f** sound in the words below. Write each word beside its definition. Please use the dictionary.

affordable	**freedom**	**pontifical**	**buff**	**phonics**	**phone**	**photograph**
suffering	**faithful**	**physician**	**puff**	**fortitude**	**fasting**	**Offertory**

______________________ pertaining to popes

______________________ able to be paid for

______________________ going without eating

______________________ picture taken with a camera

______________________ part of the Mass after the Gospel

______________________ enduring pain

______________________ doctor

______________________ loyal

______________________ a cardinal virtue

______________________ what we prize in America

______________________ to polish

______________________ to expand

DIRECTIONS: Choose the correct word from above to complete each sentence. Write the word on the line.

1. The ______________________ works in the hospital.
2. The ______________________ of the girl was in black and white.
3. Low-cost dresses are ______________________.
4. After the sermon, the priest says the ______________________ of the Mass.
5. The people were ______________________ during Lent.
6. ______________________ is a virtue.
7. The gunshot wound caused much pain and ______________________.
8. The ______________________ decree was published in Rome.
9. St. Dominic Savio remained ______________________ to the Ten Commandments.

Lesson 11 - s Sounds

Rule: The consonant **s** can have the **s** sound in **saint**, the **z** sound in **rose**, the **sh** sound in **sure**, or the **zh** sound in **pleasure**.

DIRECTIONS: Draw a line under each word in the sentences below that contains an **s**. Write **s**, **z**, **sh**, or **zh** above each underlined word to show the sound **s** makes in that word.

1. Many of my friends attend Seton Home Study School.
2. St. Elizabeth Ann Seton lived in Emmitsburg, Maryland.
3. Do not covet your neighbor's goods.
4. We are sure to overcome bad thoughts if we immediately ask Our Blessed Mother's assistance and begin to think of something else.
5. The tenth commandment forbids all desire to keep unjustly what belongs to others.
6. Each of the sacraments gives a special grace, called a sacramental grace, which helps us to carry out the purpose of that particular sacrament.
7. Throughout the Old Testament, the Chosen People looked forward to the birth of the Savior.
8. Baptism can be received only once.
9. We must receive the sacraments with the right dispositions.
10. Babies are to be baptized as soon as possible after birth.
11. The name of a saint is given in Baptism in order that the person baptized may imitate his virtues, and have him for a protector.
12. Years ago, there were many St. Dominic Savio Classroom Clubs.
13. After reading the life of Dominic Savio, we are not surprised that many young people want to follow his good example.
14. Dominic was very patient as the doctors, not knowing medical technology in 1857, bled him several times, believing that the sickness would go out of his body with the blood.
15. Where your heart is, there your treasure lies.

Lesson 12 - s Sounds

DIRECTIONS: Circle the word which completes the sentence. The correct word should have the same **s** sound as the word before the sentence.

1. **pose** Some Seton students think the study of phonics is ________________________.

   safety easy simple

2. **sum** God the Father promised Adam and Eve that He would send a ________________________.

   serpent seizure Savior

3. **miss** Thou shalt not bear false ________________________.

   lies tales witness

4. **applause** It was difficult to see Father because he was so ________________________.

   slow sick busy

5. **measure** Jesus said that where our ________________________ is, that is where our heart is also.

   soul certainty treasure

6. **sing** Dominic Savio's First Communion and Consecration to Mary marked a milestone in his ________________________ life.

   physical spiritual seasonal

7. **such** Dominic Savio knew the treacherous water in the rivers and refused to join the boys for a ________________________.

   sweet lesson swim

8. **division** The rewards in Heaven that Jesus Christ promises us are unending and ________________________.

   everlasting special immeasurable

9. **presence** St. Dominic Savio said on his deathbed, "Receive me into Thy loving bosom of Thy mercy, where I may ever sing Thy ________________________."

   praises cross scapular

10. **goodness** St. Dominic Savio loved St. John Bosco so much that he followed his every ________________________.

    successful hemisphere counsel

Lesson 13 - wh Sounds

Rule: The letters **wh** can stand for the sound of **h** as in **whole**, or for the sound of **wh** as in **whale**.

DIRECTIONS: Read the sentences and circle each word containing **wh**. Write an **h** or **wh** above the word according to the sound for which it stands.

---

1. A favorite story in the Bible is about Jonah and the whale.
2. While we are not sure, it could have been a great white whale.
3. During the storm, the captain asked Jonah, "What are you doing?"
4. The sailors on the ship decided to cast lots to find out "on whose account have we met with this misfortune?"
5. Jonah told the sailors, "I worship the Lord, the God of Heaven, Who made the sea and the dry land."
6. Jonah remained in the belly of the great white whale for three days.
7. Jonah declared, "When my soul fainted within me, I remembered the Lord."
8. The whale threw Jonah whole out of his mouth.
9. Jonah said to God, "Is not this what I said while I was still in my own country? This is why I fled."
10. "Whom do men say that I am?"
11. Jesus is wholly present in the Holy Eucharist.
12. It is a wholesome thought to pray for the dead in Purgatory.
13. John the Baptist told the people that when Christ came, He would gather the wheat into His barn, "but the chaff He will burn with unquenchable fire" (Luke 3:17).
14. The wheels of the Egyptian chariots became stuck in the mud as the waters of the Red Sea returned.
15. Christ said, "Whatever you do to the least of My people, that you do unto Me."

Lesson 14 - sh Sounds

Rule: The letters **sh**, **ci**, and **ti** can stand for the **sh** sound in words.

Letters	**Words**	**Sound**
sh	show	sh
ci	special	sh
ti	patience	sh

DIRECTIONS: Complete each sentence with a word from the list below.

temptation	distractions	Contrition	officials	revision
superstition	Confirmation	remission	omission	petition
confusion	Incarnation	unselfish	shut-ins	shun

1. In the Our Father, we say "Lead us not into ________________________."
2. The Our Father is a prayer of perfect and ________________________ love.
3. Try to avoid ________________________ in church.
4. The Act of ________________________ tells God we are sorry for our sins.
5. We should pray for the ________________________ of our country.
6. Only ignorant people believe in ________________________.
7. When will you receive the sacrament of ________________________?
8. Sin brought much ____________________ into the world.
9. The ________________________ was when God became Man at the Annunciation.
10. An indulgence gives us partial ________________________ of the punishment due to sin.
11. When a person does not do something he knows God wants him to do, he commits a sin of ________________________.
12. A ________________________ is a prayer that asks God to do something.
13. It is uncharitable to ________________________ someone for no good reason.
14. The truths of the Catholic Church are not open to ________________________.
15. Visiting ________________________ is an important work of charity.

Lesson 15 - Review

DIRECTIONS: Read the story aloud. Look up any unknown words in the dictionary.

Quest for the Holy Grail

The knights of old often went in search of the Holy Grail. The Holy Grail is a legendary sacred vessel which is identified as the chalice which Jesus used when He instituted the Sacrament of the Holy Eucharist.

The knowledge of the location of the Grail is not in the Gospels. The exact location was not known. Knights traveled across Europe to North Africa looking for the Grail. They did not have our modern techniques of travel. They went on horses and carried their goods in carts. They counted on people's charity for food and lodging. They stayed at the chateaux of other knights as they traveled.

The mystique of the Grail inspired them. Men of strong character made sacrifices to travel far from home. Even if they could not unlock the mystery and locate it, they tried. It took courage and fortitude.

The travels of the knights have been written in many folk tales, legends, and poems. Perhaps you have heard stories of Sir Galahad and King Arthur and the Knights of the Round Table. *Idylls of the King* by Sir Alfred Lord Tennyson, one of the most famous English poets, consists of twelve long narrative poems about King Arthur and his knights.

The Boston Public Library has housed fifteen famous mural paintings representing the "Quest of the Holy Grail." Look in your library for books about King Arthur.

DIRECTIONS: Fill in the blanks with words from the story.

1. ________________________ went in search of the Holy ________________________.
2. The travelers depended on others' ________________________.
3. They could not find the exact ________________________ of the Grail.
4. The ________________________ are the true stories of the life of Christ and His teachings.
5. The knights could not ________________________ the mystery.
6. The men traveled to North ________________________.
7. Such a search took ________________________ and fortitude.
8. The ________________________ of the Grail stories inspired the knights.
9. The travels of the knights have been written in many ________________________, including *Idylls of the King*.
10. Mural paintings of knights are ________________________ in the Boston Library.

Lesson 16 - Review

DIRECTIONS: Read the following words aloud.

kindly	king	black	clique	rock	marks
lack	kitten	peck	mystique	boutique	queen
question	kneel	knock	quest	quick	know
acquire	knee	Quakers	bench	choir	chateau
leech	chrism	lunch	chenille	chastity	character
chaperone	chivalry	chapel	incense	Columbus	Catholic
crude	crowd	cross	crop	corn	canoe
angels	ruffle	genuflect	game	glorious	marriage
theology	gospel	homage	generous	pontiff	phone
fireproof	phonics	phrase	staff	French	puff
freedom	faithful	sinner	rose	sure	pleasure
Seton	goods	game	else	desire	Baptism
within	whole	whale	whom	wheels	whatever
show	special	patience	shun	unselfish	revision
officials	shut	grace	temptation	sick	knight
knowledge	quicksand	Christmas	catacombs	congregation	indulgence
assistance	fasting	affordable	sacramental	white	petition

Lesson 17 - th Sounds

Rule: The letters **th** can stand for the **th** you hear in **thin** or for the **th** sound you hear in **then**.

Examples of words that sound like *then*: *the*, *this*, *that*, *there*, *these*, *they*, *thou*, and *thus*.

Examples of words that sound like *thin*: *think*, *thing*, *thank*, *thick*, *thirty*, and *threw*.

DIRECTIONS: Write each word beside its definition. Then write **thin** or **then** to show the sound that **th** has in that word.

Faith	wither	Ruth	Nazareth	St. Matthew
Catholic	youth	three	St. Timothy	God the Father

Definition	Word	Sound
the First Person of the Blessed Trinity	________________	______
young people	________________	______
the number of days Jonah was in the whale	________________	______
a theological virtue	________________	______
the city where Jesus lived as a Boy	________________	______
she followed her mother-in-law	________________	______
what we are proud to be	________________	______
a Gospel writer	________________	______
a close friend of St. Paul	________________	______
when a flower dies	________________	______

DIRECTIONS: Please complete the following sentences with words from the list above.

1. The __________________ Divine Persons are perfectly equal to One Another because All are One and the same God.
2. Jesus met __________________ while he was collecting taxes.
3. St. Joseph took Mary and Jesus back to __________________ after they had lived in Egypt.
4. There is a famous painting of __________________ and Naomi as they gleaned the wheat from the fields of Boaz.
5. St. Dominic Savio is considered a patron of __________________.

Lesson 18 - sc Sounds

Rule: The letters **sc** can stand for the **s** sound in **science**, or the **sk** sound in **scamper**, or for the **sh** sound in **conscious**. When **s** ends a syllable, and **c** begins the next syllable, each letter is pronounced as in **discard.**

DIRECTIONS: Circle each word which has an **sc**. Write in the blank **s**, **sk**, or **sh** according to the sound the **sc** stands for. Write **s/c** if the **sc** is divided between two syllables.

---

1. _____ Michelangelo was a famous Catholic sculptor who carved the beautiful *Pieta* statue at St. Peter's in Rome.
2. _____ Many scientific discoveries were made by famous Catholic priests, such as St. Albert and Duns Scotus.
3. _____ We homeschooling students need to be conscientious about doing our schoolwork in a timely manner.
4. _____ Song at the Scaffold is the story of French nuns during the French Revolution.
5. _____ Jesus told the parable of the farmer who scattered seed on various types of soil.
6. _____ The scent of incense during Benediction helps us to think about the Kingship of Jesus Christ.
7. _____ When the cruel soldiers put the scarlet cloak on Jesus, they began to mock Him as a king.
8. _____ The chief sins against charity are hatred of our neighbor, envy, sloth, and scandal.
9. _____ St. Dominic Savio was not scared when the other boys laughed at him for being good.
10. _____ Jesus taught the people that God the Father would listen to their prayers, just as a father would give his son bread and not a stone, would give him fish and not a serpent, and would give him an egg and not a scorpion.
11. _____ At the time of Jesus, scourging was a legal punishment.
12. _____ An Egyptian professional writer was called a scribe. These people were wealthy because very few others could read or write.
13. _____ The Jewish scribe in New Testament times was the scholar and intellectual of the Jewish community.
14. _____ Herod scowled at the news of the coming of the Messiah.
15. _____ Jesus scolded the Pharisees for their love of self and their love of signs of respect.

Lesson 19 - gn Sound

Rule: The letters **gn** usually stand for the sound of **n** as in **sign**.

DIRECTIONS: Read each sentence aloud and circle the words with a **gn**.

1. Aaron stretched out his hand and, with his staff, he struck the dust of the earth, and gnats came upon man and beast. The dust of the earth was turned into gnats throughout the land of Egypt.
2. After Jesus cured the ten lepers, only one, a Samaritan, returned to give thanks. Jesus said, "Has no one been found to return and give glory to God except this foreigner?"
3. The words of a Slovak hymn are "Little King, so fair and sweet, See us gathered at Thy feet; Be Thou Sovereign of our school, It shall prosper 'neath Thy rule. We will be Thy subjects true, Brave to suffer, brave to do; All our hearts to Thee we bring, Take them, keep them, Little King."
4. The unusual blue color in the design on the dress of the miraculous painting of Our Lady of Guadalupe cannot be duplicated in this world. This is also said about the red in the miraculous painting of Our Lady of Good Counsel. Photographs cannot accurately convey the color, though millions of shades of color can be reproduced.
5. Cologne is a city in Germany, a chief industrial, commercial, and cultural center on the Rhine River.
6. The Cologne Cathedral is the city's most famous landmark, a magnificent Gothic structure with two 515-foot towers, beautiful stained-glass windows, and incredible works of art. It is the largest Gothic church in Northern Europe.
7. Gnostics were people who lived before Jesus Christ and up to the fifth century, and who believed they knew all the mysteries of the universe.
8. The chief priests and the scribes wanted to capture Jesus. Luke records in his Gospel, in chapter 20, that they "sent spies, who should feign themselves just, that they might take hold of Him in His words, that they might deliver Him up to the authority and power of the governor."
9. In the Old Testament, Job spoke to his friends about a group of men who were so hungry that they "gnawed in the wilderness," eating grass and the roots of juniper trees.
10. When Jesus was speaking to the centurion in the Gospel of Matthew, He spoke of those who had faith and would be saved in the Kingdom of Heaven. He spoke also about those who would be "cast into darkness. There shall be weeping and gnashing of teeth."

Lesson 20 - r Sound

Rule: The **r** sound may be expressed by the letters **rh** such as in **rhyme**, and by **wr** as in **wrist**.

DIRECTIONS: Read the sentences below aloud. Underline the words with **rh**. Circle the words with **wr**.

1. St. Paul explained to the Corinthians that he suffered greatly as an apostle of Jesus Christ: "Thrice was I beaten with rods; once I was stoned; thrice I suffered shipwreck."
2. Jesus told the parable of the laborers in the vineyard. The master of the vineyard agreed to pay them all the same amount, but those who had worked all day complained. He answered them, saying, "Friend, I do thee no wrong. Did you not agree with me for [the wage]?"
3. Many of the Jews of Jericho did not like Zacheus because he was a rich tax collector. When Zacheus stood in front of Jesus, he said, "Behold, Lord, the half of my goods I give to the poor; if I have wronged any man of anything, I restore him fourfold."
4. Moses was with God forty days and forty nights. He neither ate bread nor drank water, and he wrote upon the tables [of stone] the ten words [Commandments] of the covenant.
5. Jacob, in the Book of Genesis, had a vision of angels, but he also was forced to wrestle with one of them all night. In the morning, the angel blessed him, and told him God now wanted him to be called Israel.
6. Gideon wanted a sign from God that he was to lead the Jewish people. He asked that, while the floor was dry all night, God would send dew upon a fleece of wool. "And it was so. Rising before day, wringing the fleece, he was able to fill a vessel with the dew."
7. During Advent, our family likes to make an Advent Wreath, to celebrate the four thousand years the Jewish people waited for the Messiah to come.
8. The wren is one of many small singing birds which God has made to entertain us, both in song and in beauty.
9. When the soldiers nailed Jesus on the Cross, they wrenched His arms to reach the nail holes they had previously made.
10. Rhode Island is the smallest state in the United States, and was the last of the thirteen colonies to become a state.
11. A good poem has both rhyme, usually of the last words in a line, and rhythm, a pattern of stressed and unstressed syllables.
12. Rheumatic fever is a disease which used to occur fairly frequently in children and young adults, with fever, pains, and swelling around the joints.
13. Rheumatism is a condition usually in older persons, with pain and swelling in the joints. Persons with this disease often complain when the weather is humid or rainy.
14. The Rhine, being 824 miles long, is a chief river of Western Europe. The Rhone, another river in Europe which is 505 miles long, is a major supplier of hydroelectric power for the people in Switzerland and France. Can you find these rivers on a map?

Lesson 21 - ear Sounds

Rule: The letters **ear** can stand for three sounds:

ear sound as in **clear**
air sound as in **pear**
ur sound as in **pearl**

DIRECTIONS: Read each sentence below and underline each **ear** word. Then write each word you underlined in the correct list on the next page.

---

1. Most litanies start with "Christ hear us, Christ graciously hear us."
2. Mary was earning money at the local store to help support her sister in the convent.
3. It was clear to Pope Gregory VII that King Henry IV of northern Italy was not repentant, since he continued to defy the laws of the Church.
4. The soldier wanted to prove Jesus was dead on the Cross, so he opened His side with a spear.
5. In the early Church, people did not receive Communion every day, but today, everyone has the opportunity to receive daily Communion.
6. In the liturgical year, we celebrate the feasts of hundreds of saints.
7. After His Resurrection, Jesus appeared to Mary Magdalene.
8. A person commits the sin of detraction when he, without a good reason, makes known the hidden faults of another. This is commonly called "smearing the good name of another."
9. When the Jewish high priest heard Jesus declare He was the Son of God, the high priest began to tear his garments, saying, "He has blasphemed!"
10. Peter was so fearful that when he was asked if he were a friend of Jesus, Peter denied it three times.
11. *The Hound of Heaven* is a famous Catholic poem about the fact that God wants us and loves us so much, that He goes to great lengths to search us out, in the midst of our tears and "running laughter."
12. The Christmas song, "Partridge in a Pear Tree," is about the twelve days of Christmas during which some people give small gifts each day.
13. As the evil soldiers of Herod approached near to the Holy Family, Joseph fled with Mary and Jesus to Egypt.
14. Jesus asks us to bear our problems in prayer and sacrifice, just as He bore His cross.

Lesson 22 - ear Sounds

DIRECTIONS: Write the **ear** words from the previous page in the proper column.

ear as in **clear**	**ear** as in **pear**	**ear** as in **pearl**
______________	______________	______________
______________	______________	______________
______________	______________	______________
______________		______________
______________		
______________		
______________		

DIRECTIONS: Write an **ear** word for each the following definitions.

1. to gain knowledge ______________
2. hair on the face of a man ______________
3. ornaments for a lady's ears ______________
4. close ______________
5. a name for someone who is loved ______________
6. tired ______________

DIRECTIONS: Read the sentences aloud. Circle the **ear** words.

1. "Heaven was shut up three years and six months when there was a great famine throughout all the earth" (Luke 4:25).
2. "The multitudes pressed upon Him to hear the Word of God" (Luke 5:1).
3. "Fear not: from henceforth thou shalt be fishers of men" (Luke: 5:10).
4. "I am the true vine, and My Father is the husbandman. Every branch in Me that bears not fruit, He will take away: and every one that bears fruit, He will purge it, that it may bring forth more fruit" (John 15:1).
5. "Cast first the beam out of your own eye, and then thou shalt see clearly to take out the mote from thy brother's eye" (Luke 6:42).

Lesson 23 - air Sound

Rule: The **air** sound can be spelled **are** as in **care**, or **air** as in **hair**.

DIRECTIONS: Read the sentences aloud. Underline each word in which you see **are**. Circle each word in which you see **air**.

1. Joseph brought a pair of doves to the temple at the Presentation of Jesus.
2. Many holy women stared in disbelief when they saw Jesus on the Cross.
3. Some of the Jewish children were scared as they walked through the Red Sea on the dry land between the walls of water.
4. At a holy church in Rome, Catholics ascend the stairs on their knees as they approach the holy place.
5. Several of our Seton families live on dairy farms; the students do their chores, milking the cows between their assignments.
6. St. Martin of Tours shared his cloak with a poor beggar, who turned out to be Jesus Christ Himself.
7. On Good Friday, the altar boys strip the altar bare in remembrance of the death of Jesus.
8. Whenever you go on an airplane, do you ever pray for all the people flying in the plane with you?
9. St. Dominic Savio teaches us to be careful about the things we see with our eyes, and the things that we hear with our ears.
10. The Blessed Virgin Mary is the purest, the fairest, and the holiest of all God's creatures.
11. He who fares well in this world may not fare well in the next.
12. Jesus died on the Cross to repair for the sins of mankind, and to open the gates of heaven.
13. Spare, O God, in mercy, spare the souls in Purgatory!
14. O St. Rita, you did share the sorrowful passion of Jesus by bearing the wounds of Christ in the stigmata.

Lesson 24 - ild, ind, ost, & old Sounds

DIRECTIONS: Read aloud the sentences below, then complete the unfinished word in each sentence by writing the letters **ild** or **ind**.

1. Mothers often must rem____________ children about special prayers on First Friday.
2. The Holy Childhood Association promotes devotion among children for the Ch____________ Jesus.
3. The bl____________ man, Bartimeus, would not keep quiet, but cried louder and louder until Jesus called him to Him.
4. When the apostles could not cast a devil out of a man, Jesus said, "This k____________ is not cast out except by prayer and fasting."
5. Some of the effects of the seven gifts of the Holy Spirit are the twelve fruits of the Holy Spirit, such as joy, peace, patience, goodness, and m____________ ness.

DIRECTIONS: Read aloud the sentences below, then circle the words in each sentence which contain **ost** or **old**.

1. Most Sacred Heart of Jesus, I implore, make me love Thee more and more.
2. Joseph was sold by his brothers to the Egyptians because they were jealous.
3. The elevation of the Host is the most sacred part of the Mass.
4. The three kings brought to the King of the Universe the kingly gifts of gold, frankincense, and myrrh.
5. Come Holy Ghost, Creator Blest, and in my heart take up Thy rest.
6. "And the soldiers led Him away into the court of the palace" (Mark 15:16).
7. Anna had no children, so she prayed, "Oh Lord of Hosts . . . if you will give to your servant a man child, I will give him to the Lord" (Kings 1:11).
8. Our postman does his utmost to deliver our mail even in cold, icy weather.
9. "But they, holding Jesus, led him to Caiphas the high priest" (Matthew 26:57).
10. "Joseph of Arimathea . . . went in boldly to Pilate and begged the body of Jesus" (Mark 15:43).

Lesson 25 - Syllables

Rule: Words have one or more syllables. Each syllable has at least one vowel. A word has as many syllables as it has vowel sounds.

DIRECTIONS: Read the word list below. Check the dictionary for pronunciation if necessary. Write the words in the appropriate column.

infamy	church	song	good	bad	bell
simple	pilgrim	wheat	grace	belief	signature
Satan	Gothic	vespers	religion	piety	communion
	triangle	devotion	alb	incense	

One Syllable	Two Syllables	Three Syllables
__________	__________	__________
__________	__________	__________
__________	__________	__________
__________	__________	__________
__________	__________	__________
__________	__________	__________
__________	__________	__________
__________		

DIRECTIONS: Use a word from the list above for each definition.

__________ white robe worn by a priest

__________ a three-cornered shape

__________ metal instrument that rings

__________ a person's written name

__________ a melody with words

__________ another name for the devil

__________ a type of architecture

__________ a crop used to make bread

__________ the life of the soul

__________ a truth of Christian doctrine

Lesson 26 - Syllables

Rule: When a single consonant comes between two vowels in a word, the word is divided **after** the consonant if the first vowel is **short**. Example: **mŏd | est**

Dictionaries often identify **short** vowels with a "breve" (˘) over the letter: **ă, ĕ, ĭ, ŏ, ŭ**

Rule: When a single consonant comes between two vowels in a word, the word is usually divided **before** the consonant if the first vowel is **long**. Example: **pī | lot**

Dictionaries often identify **long** vowels with a line (¯) over the letter: **ā, ē, ī, ō, ū**

---

short vowel	**long vowel**
seven	Jesus
sĕv | en	**Jē | sus**

DIRECTIONS: Study the rules above. Divide the words below into syllables, using a slash (/) between syllables.

Bible	Bi / ble	Latin	________
lady	________	Magi	________
medal	________	papal	________
power	________	relics	________
Satan	________	mercy	________
damage	________	tunic	________
Penance	________	Easter	________
visit	________	canon	________
sinner	________	melon	________
reward	________	lawful	________
decade	________	pity	________
garden	________	amen	________
preface	________	Scribes	________
malice	________	parish	________
lunar	________	moral	________

DIRECTIONS: Remember that **e** at the end of a word is often silent. Circle the words in the list above that end in a silent **e.**

Lesson 27 - Sounds Review

DIRECTIONS: Read the list words. Use the words to fill in the blanks in the sentences below. Can you spell them from memory?

church	wrapped	rage	rosary	design
scientists	thought	when	knew	

A group of ____________________ set out to examine the Shroud of Turin because they ____________________ they could prove it to be a fake. ____________________ they reached the ____________________ where the Shroud was kept, the pastor, their host, asked them to say the ____________________ with him. He ____________________ Mary would guide them to the truth. The men were filled with ____________________. Most of them hated religion. They believed religion was dangerous to intellectual development.

The men were quick to say they wouldn't pray. They came only to look at the Shroud. The priest showed this special treasure to them. They could see the shape or ____________________ of a human body in the cloth. After close examination, they came away believing that the Shroud of Turin was really the cloth Christ was ____________________ in while He was in the tomb.

DIRECTIONS: Use the list words above to answer the questions below.

1. Which word has two consonants that sound like **n**? ____________________
2. Which word has a **g** that sounds like **j**? ____________________
3. Which word has an **s** that sounds like **z**? ____________________
4. Which word has a **wh** that sounds like **w**? ____________________
5. Which word has a **gn** that sounds like **n**? ____________________

Lesson 28 - Review

DIRECTIONS: Imagine that you were at Fatima when the miracle of the sun happened. When you came home, your friends were asking you questions. Be sure to answer the questions with complete sentences. Use the list words in your answers.

carefully	festivities	physician	kind	wrath	rheumatism
cared	near	mother	conscious	clear	queen

Friend: What was it like in the village the night before the expected miracle?

You: ____

____ .

Friend: How close did you get to the children?

You: ____

____ .

Friend: What kind of a day was it?

You: ____

____ .

Friend: How did you walk in the fields?

You: ____

____ .

Friend: Who did the children say they saw?

You: ____

____ .

Friend: Who examined the people who were cured?

You: ____

____ .

Friend: What were some of the diseases that were cured?

You: ____

____ .

DIRECTIONS: Reread your sentences aloud for correct pronunciation. Do they answer the question? Do they start with a capital letter? Do they end with correct punctuation?

Lesson 29 - ai & ay Sounds

Rule: The double vowels **ai** can stand for the long sound of **a** that you hear in the word **hail**.

The letters **ay** also can stand for the long sound of **a**.

In the dictionary, the long sound is represented by a line above the letter: **ā, ē, ī, ō, ū**

Letters	**Words**	**Sound**
ai	hail	**ā**
ay	layman	**ā**

DIRECTIONS: Read the list of words aloud. Fill in the blanks with the correct word.

bay	nails	say	Hail	layman	rain
hay	failure	spray	main	payment	tail

1. The Roman soldiers put ______________________ in Christ's hands and feet.
2. Can you ______________________ the ______________________ Mary?
3. When Christ died, there was a heavy ______________________.
4. Baby Jesus slept on ______________________ in the manger.
5. The power ______________________ left us without electricity.
6. A ______________________ of water from the bay hit me as I walked over the bridge.
7. Samson caught three hundred foxes, and coupled them tail to ______________________.
8. The ______________________ helped the priests in the parish retreat.
9. The ______________________ reason John made his credit card ______________________ on time was to avoid interest charges.

DIRECTIONS: Write the list words in the proper column.

ai sounds like **ā**	**ay** sounds like **ā**
______________________	______________________
______________________	______________________
______________________	______________________
______________________	______________________
______________________	______________________
______________________	______________________

Lesson 30 - ai & ay Sounds

Rule: If a syllable has two vowels, usually the first vowel is long and the second vowel is silent.

The letters **ay** and **ai** usually have the long **a** sound (**ā**).

The long vowel sound is often represented by a line above the letter: **ā, ē, ī, ō, ū**

DIRECTIONS: Read the sentences aloud. Spell the words correctly by writing **ai** or **ay** in the blanks.

---

1. The d ________ly trip was hardest in the r________n.
2. Children like to pl________ in the h________ in the fields.
3. Will you be going aw________ on the tr________n tomorrow?
4. What d________ did it r________n?
5. Did you s________ the l________ man hammered the n________ ls into the pew?
6. The m________n street of the town was cleaned every d_________ .
7. The dog wagged his t________l as he w________ted for us.
8. They had to b________l water from the boat after the s________l fell on the deck.
9. The p________ment of the bill was late.
10. We rem________ned in the hotel because of the storm.
11. The delivery of the gr________ suit was del________ed.
12. Midw________ down the tr________l, the road was blocked.

DIRECTIONS: Use these words to answer the questions below.

---

rain stain hay day

What would you call a water spot? ________________________________

What's the opposite of night? ________________________________

DIRECTIONS: Read the sentences below, then circle the **ay** and **ai** words

---

1. "They have beaten me, but I was not sensible of pain" (Proverbs 23:35).
2. "Jesus . . . You, by the hands of wicked men, have been crucified and slain" (Acts 2:23).
3. Abraham asked God not to "slay the just with the wicked" (Genesis 18:25).
4. King Saul asked that the shepherd boy, David, be brought to him because David was "skillful in playing the harp" (I King 16:16).
5. "O Come All Ye Faithful" is a favorite Christmas hymn.

Lesson 31- ee & ei Sounds

Rule: If a syllable has two vowels, usually the first vowel is long and the second vowel is silent. The letters **ee** and **ei** usually stand for the long **e** sound.

Letters	Words	Sounds
ee	bee	ē
ei	ceiling	ē

DIRECTIONS: Read aloud the words in the list. Use your dictionary to find meanings of words you do not know. Then circle the letters that make a long **e** sound and write each word in the proper column below.

succeeded	agree	steep	ceiling	receive	keeping
wheel	green	needles	receipts	protein	deceitful
free	deceive	reel	perceive	glee	conceive

ee words	**ei** words
________________	________________
________________	________________
________________	________________
________________	________________
________________	________________
________________	________________
________________	________________
________________	________________
________________	
________________	

DIRECTIONS: Read the sentences aloud. Circle the **ee** and **ei** words.

1. The ceiling in the Sistine Chapel in the Vatican is covered by paintings by Michelangelo.
2. In Holy Communion, we receive the Body and Blood of Jesus Christ.
3. The young lady could not perceive the conceit of her friend.
4. God can neither deceive nor be deceived.
5. "Little King so Fair and Sweet" is a song to praise Jesus, especially during our annual dedication ceremony to the Infant of Prague.

Lesson 32 - ee & ei Sounds

Rule: If a syllable has two vowels, usually the first vowel is long and the second vowel is silent. The vowels **ee** and **ei** have the long **e** sound that you hear in **bee** and **receive**.

DIRECTIONS: Complete each sentence with a word from Lesson 31.

1. Did you ______________________________ to sell the house?
2. The new ______________________________ helped in steering the bike.
3. They painted the ______________________________ white and the walls blue.
4. He ______________________________ in finishing the book he was writing.
5. The ______________________________ hill was the cause of many accidents.
6. She is ______________________________ the statue of the Infant of Prague.
7. Mary bought new ______________________________ to do her sewing.
8. "______________________________ ye the Holy Spirit. Whose sins you shall forgive, they are forgiven. Whose sins you shall retain are retained."
9. St. Patrick is always painted in ________________________ robes.
10. Vitamins and __________________________ are essential for a healthy body.
11. The ______________________________ devil lied to Eve in the Garden of Paradise.
12. The money and ______________________________ from the sale of Nativity sets were given to our pastor.

More words with ē sound

whee	**neither**
tree	either
seem	conceivable
creek	inconceivable
free	conceit

Lesson 33 - oa, oe, & ow Sounds

Rule: If a syllable has two vowels, usually the first vowel is long and the second vowel is silent. The vowels **oa** and **oe** can stand for the long sound of **o**. The letters **ow** usually have the long **o** sound. The long **o** sound is often written like this in a dictionary: **ō**.

Letters	Words	Sound
oa	float	**ō**
oe	toe	**ō**
ow	grow	**ō**

DIRECTIONS: Read the sentences aloud. Circle the words that have the long **o** sound.

1. The boat would not float.
2. There was a bow on the toe of the slipper.
3. Dad's new machine could blow the snow off the driveway.
4. Can you grow oats in that field?
5. The coat had a row of black buttons.
6. He took an oath that he did not steal the farmer's hoe.
7. Will you show me the blue boat?
8. Mary will give the bowling ball to the bowler.
9. The car cast a long shadow on the road.
10. The loaves of bread were used for toast.

DIRECTIONS: Write the **oa**, **oe**, and **ow** words from the sentences above in the correct column below.

ow	oe	oa
______	______	______
______	______	______
______		______
______		______
______		______
______		______
______		______
______		______
______		______

Lesson 34 - oa, oe, & ow Sounds

Rule: If a syllable has two vowels, usually the first vowel is long and the second vowel is silent. The letters **oa**, **oe**, and **ow** have the long **o** sound, as in **so**. Note that **ow**, however, can have another sound, as in **now** and **cow**.

DIRECTIONS: Read aloud the following sentences and underline <u>all</u> the words with the **ō** sound. Note that *Porres* and other words with **o** followed by **r** do not contain the **ō** sound.

---

1. St. Martin de Porres lived in the crowded streets of Lima, Peru, long ago.
2. As a young boy, Martin had to stand on tiptoe to lift the gold, hand-shaped knockers on the doors of the rich Spanish homes in Peru.
3. The Spanish girls of Lima wore gold-braided dresses, tight at their waists with their skirts billowing around their feet.
4. There was much prejudice in Lima at the time of Martin de Porres. Martin had an African mother, and was told to "keep to his own kind."
5. Little Martin lived in fear, loneliness, and pain, but he did know the Blessed Mother would not reject him.
6. Martin would go down to the docks of Lima to help the poor African slaves who came off the boats.
7. Martin was beaten many times by his mother because he gave their food and money to the poor. He learned to protect himself from the constant blows.
8. When Martin lived for a few years with a rich uncle, he received an excellent education; he learned about the human body, about animals, and about plants and flowers and how they grow.
9. Martin spent a few years as an apprentice to a doctor in Lima. Martin learned to heal wounds and diseases with plants and herbs and to recognize diseases in the young and old, friend or foe.
10. At the Church of Santo Domingo in Lima, Martin met all types of people at daily Mass, the rich and the poor, the Indians, the Spanish and the Africans. The woes of all the people weighed heavily on poor Martin.
11. Martin joined the Dominican monastery, and continued to help the poor with food and medical help for those coming off the boats.
12. Martin showed the poor children of Lima how to grow an orchard from seeds and saplings. The orchard for and by the poor children of Lima became very famous. For many years, Martin showed the people how to plant, cultivate, and harvest fig, olive, and orange orchards, which became the common property of the poor. Some of the orchards planted by Martin in the sixteenth century still exist.

Lesson 35 - ai, ay, ee, ei, oa, oe, & ow Sounds

DIRECTIONS: Read aloud the paragraph below. Please fill in one of the following missing pair of letters: **ai, ay, ee, ei, oa, oe,** and **ow**.

The d_____nty little girl came in out of the r_____n. She looked out the window and saw the trees sw_____ in the wind. As the temperature dropped, she wondered if it was going to sn_____. As she sat by the window, sn_____ flakes began to fall. They covered the gr_____n grass. She could hardly see the church st_____ple as the storm increased.

Mother said, "There will be a del_____ in the m_____l delivery tod_____ because of the weather. Mr. Jones, the m_____lman, will have a hard time driving up that st_____p hill. The r_____d is covered with ice." She expl_____ned, "He likes to b_____st that the mail always gets through. I think that is conc_____t on his part."

The girl took some candy from the b_____l on the tr_____. Then she picked up her n_____dlework to k_____p herself busy. M_____ be it will stop sn_____ing soon, she thought. She put on the light to s_____ better.

They would not rec_____ve any m_____l today, she thought as she kicked the thr_____ rug with her t_____. She went into the kitchen to eat, and saw that her cat had gone to sl_____p.

DIRECTIONS: Read aloud the following sentences, then circle any words which have the letters **ai**, **ay**, **ee**, **ei**, **oa**, **oe**, or **ow**.

Straightaway in the morning, after holding a consultation with the ancients, the scribes and the whole council bound Jesus, led Him away and delivered Him to Pilate. And Pilate asked Him, "Art Thou the King of the Jews?" Christ answered, saying to him, "Thou sayest it."

Lesson 36 - Review

DIRECTIONS: Read aloud the paragraphs below. Point out some words with a long vowel sound.

1. When Christ appeared to the apostles in the Upper Room, St. Thomas was not with them. Upon his return, they told him about Our Lord's visit. Thomas was doubtful. Thomas said, "Unless I put my fingers in the nail holes in His hands and my hand in the wound in His side, I will not believe."
2. After Our Lord's Ascension, the Holy Ghost descended upon the apostles. That day is known as Pentecost Sunday, the birthday of the Church. The Holy Ghost appeared in tongues of fire. He infused His fruits and gifts into their souls. The apostles gained courage to leave the Upper Room. They went out to spread the words of Christ. The apostles, with the grace of the Holy Ghost, converted many people.
3. Therefore I say to you, be not solicitous for your life, what you shall eat, nor for your body, what you shall put on. Is not the life more than the meat, and the body more than the raiment? Behold the birds of the air, for they neither sow, nor do they reap, nor gather into barns; and your heavenly Father feeds them. Are you not of much more value than they? And which of you by taking thought, can add to his stature one cubit? And for raiment, why are you solicitous? Consider the lilies of the field, how they grow: they labour not, neither do they spin. But I say to you, that not even Solomon in all his glory was arrayed as one of these. And if the grass of the field, which is today, and tomorrow is cast into the oven, God doth so clothe: how much more you, O ye of little faith?.....(Mt. 6:25)

Lesson 37 - ei & ey Sounds

Rule: The letters **ei** sometimes have the long **a** sound. The letters **ey** also sometimes have a long **a** sound.

Letters	Words	Sound
ei	veiled	ā
ey	survey	ā

DIRECTIONS: Read aloud the sentences below. Circle the words that use **ei** or **ey** to make the long **a** sound.

1. Christ the King reigns in Heaven.
2. They put a new veil over the Tabernacle.
3. Our factory uses a conveyor belt to move the boxes along for the workers to pack.
4. Did they obey the command of the reigning king?
5. The hunter's prey was the tundra reindeer.
6. John will survey the property tomorrow.
7. What conveyance did you use to get here?
8. Veronica's veil, with the image of the face of Jesus, is in Rome.
9. When St. Dominic Savio was sick, they bled his veins.
10. Feign, meaning to pretend, is a word we don't use often, but it does appear in literature.
11. A feint is a pretense, or false attack; it is a phrase used in speaking of military strategy or boxing.
12. Deign means to come down, to condescend to give something. As creatures of God, we sometimes ask God to "deign" to give us our request.
13. Will you convey the news that the Pilgrim Virgin statue is coming to our parish?

DIRECTIONS: Write the words from the above sentences in the proper column.

ei		ey
______	______	______
______	______	______
______	______	______
______	______	______
	______	______
		______

DIRECTIONS: Write the correct word from the list above next to the definitions below.

______ hunted animal

______ animal with long antlers

______ to rule

______ covering for a lady's hair

Lesson 38 - ea Sounds

Rule: The letters **ea** may have a long **a** sound as in **break**, a short **e** sound as in **dread**, or a long **e** sound as in **reader.**

Letters	Words	Sound
ea	break	long a (**ā**)
ea	dread	short e (**ĕ**)
ea	reader	long e (**ē**)

DIRECTIONS: Read the following sentences aloud. Draw a line under the words that have the letters **ea**.

1. The white smoke signaling that a new pope had been elected came from the Vatican chimney at daybreak.
2. The martyr, St. Thomas More, was beheaded by Henry VIII.
3. St. Michael and the good angels defeated Lucifer and the bad angels.
4. Sweat poured from the men who pulled the wagons up the hill.
5. The outbreak of World War II stranded many Americans in Germany.
6. Sister Mary Ann measured the children for uniforms.
7. The people in Ireland concealed their priests in haystacks during the British oppression.
8. The Blessed Sacrament is our greatest Treasure.
9. Always remember to eat breakfast.
10. Put the hymn books underneath the organ.
11. Some students think that home schooling is easy.
12. “For though I should walk in the midst of the shadow of death, I will fear no evil” (Psalm 22).

DIRECTIONS: Put the words you underlined under the correct sound below.

ĕ	ē	ā
____________	____________	____________
____________	____________	____________
____________	____________	____________
____________	____________	
____________	____________	
____________	____________	

Lesson 39 - ea Sounds

DIRECTIONS: Read aloud the sentences below . Find the **ea** word in each sentence below. Underline the word. Circle the sound it makes at the right.

1. Bacon and eggs make a good breakfast.	ā	ĕ	ē
2. He likes steak and eggs.	ā	ĕ	ē
3. Do you like to teach?	ā	ĕ	ē
4. She spread the blanket on the ground.	ā	ĕ	ē
5. *A Man for All Seasons* is a an inspiring play.	ā	ĕ	ē
6. The weather is very cold for spring.	ā	ĕ	ē
7. Many martyrs were beheaded.	ā	ĕ	ē
8. Did you see Bishop Sheen preach?	ā	ĕ	ē
9. Joseph likes jam on bread.	ā	ĕ	ē
10. The captain kept the ship on a steady course.	ā	ĕ	ē
11. A new house is usually neat.	ā	ĕ	ē
12. The priest is very easygoing.	ā	ĕ	ē
13. The campers awoke at daybreak.	ā	ĕ	ē
14. Mother washed the whites in bleach.	ā	ĕ	ē
15. Are you ready to go to church?	ā	ĕ	ē

Check your work; look up any word in the dictionary that you did not understand.

DIRECTIONS: Read the following sentences aloud. Circle the words with the vowels **ea**.

1. An angel of the Lord descended from Heaven. And there was a great earthquake. The guards became as dead men. The angel rolled back the stone. At daybreak, Mary Magdalen came to see the sepulchre.

2. To St. Joan of Arc we sing, "Break the yoke that burdens France and crown your king. O blessed Maid, the chant we raise that tells the meaning of thy praise: Thou teachest us the lesson grand of love for God and fatherland."

Lesson 40 - au & aw Sounds

Rule: A digraph consists of two vowels blended together to form a new single sound, such as **au** in faucet. The letters **au** and **aw** sound the same in words like **faucet** and **shawl**.

DIRECTIONS: Read aloud the sentences below. Complete the words with **au** or **aw**.

1. Mother crocheted me a new sh______l.
2. Mary broke the s______cer when she washed the dishes.
3. The screw for the f______cet was in the dr______er.
4. The l______n was full of ______tumn leaves.
5. He had to withdr______ the money to contribute to a worthy c______se.
6. Did you th______ out the str______berries for dinner?
7. The g______ky little f______n was very ______kward when he stood.
8. Joseph bought a new ______tomobile.
9. He returned the car bec______se it was fl______ed.
10. You should be c______tious about judging people.
11. The ______dience appl______ded the ______thor as he read his book.
12. Did you get an ______tographed copy of Russell's book?

DIRECTIONS: Write a word from the sentences above in front of the correct definition.

1. ________________________ to take out
2. ________________________ season that begins in September
3. ________________________ a fruit
4. ________________________ signature of an author
5. ________________________ to defrost
6. ________________________ piece of china that goes under a cup

Lesson 41 - ie Sounds

Rule: The letters **ie** can sound like long **e** or long **i**.

Letters	Word	Sound
ie	p**ie**	ī
ie	f**ie**ld	ē

DIRECTIONS: Read the words below aloud. Then write each word on the line before its definition.

1. chief ____________________ to cover, to protect
2. pie ____________________ head
3. field ____________________ dessert with crust and filling
4. shield ____________________ clothing men wear around neck
5. tie ____________________ attempted to do
6. windshield ____________________ short
7. brief ____________________ places used for manufacturing
8. tried ____________________ level land
9. factories ____________________ a false statement
10. lie ____________________ window at the front of a car

DIRECTIONS: Use the words above to fill in the blanks below.

1. Mary ____________________ to finish her work on time.
2. The ____________________ on the car was very dirty.
3. The children walked through the ____________________ of grass.
4. The police ____________________ helped the children learn safety rules.
5. Joe had to ____________________ his eyes from the sun.
6. Apple ____________________ is my favorite dessert.
7. The priest gave a ____________________ sermon on the hot Sunday.
8. Did you buy that ____________________ to match your suit?
9. It is a sin to tell a ____________________, Father Burns said.
10. Many men work in automobile ____________________.

Lesson 42 - ie Sounds

Rule: The letters **ie** sometimes sound like the long **i** in **dignified**; this follows the rule that the first vowel is long and the second vowel is silent.

Sometimes **ie** sounds like long **e** in **brief**; these words below do not follow the usual rule.

ie as ī	**ie** as ē	
untie	disbelief	piece
dignified	windshield	grief
tried	brief	relief
applied	shrieked	achieve
verified	chief	thief
lied	field	

DIRECTIONS: Write some of the list words above in a sentence. Use the dictionary if you do not know the meaning.

---

1. ______________________________

2. ______________________________

3. ______________________________

4. ______________________________

5. ______________________________

6. ______________________________

7. ______________________________

8. ______________________________

9. ______________________________

10. ______________________________

Lesson 43 - Review

DIRECTIONS: The words in the list below have sounds you have studied. Use the words from the list to complete the sentences below. Use the dictionary for any words you do not understand.

automobile	Easter	unified	lied	believe	yeast	grief
countries	ready	stories	steam	eastward	seaside	claw
awesome	head	paused	bread	Sunday	Great	say

1. Jesus gave thanks, took ______________________, blessed it and said, "This is My Body."
2. Mother boiled two dozen eggs for the ______________________ basket.
3. Gregorian Chant is named after Gregory the ______________________.
4. We must go to Mass on ______________________.
5. The man ______________________ about stealing the money.
6. Are you ______________________ to leave yet?
7. How many ______________________ did you visit on your European trip?
8. I like the ______________________ of Hans Christian Anderson.
9. The ______________________ came out of the iron when I plugged it into the outlet.
10. There was ______________________ in the nation when President Lincoln was shot.
11. Mary saw the lobster's ______________________ move in the water tank.
12. The crowd stood at the ______________________ to hear Jesus speak from the boat.
13. We put flour and ______________________ in our new breadmaker.
14. The attack by the English ______________________ the people in the American colonies.
15. The pope has a special bullet-proof ______________________ to ride around Vatican square.
16. The ______________________ winds blew the boat off course.
17. The veterans ______________________ for a moment to pray for the dead soldiers.
18. The sun setting over the Blue Ridge mountains was an ______________________ sight.
19. The pope, the Vicar of Christ on earth, is the ______________________ of the Roman Catholic Church.
20. Did you ______________________ your prayers?

Lesson 44 - Review

DIRECTIONS: Read aloud the following words. Then write 10 words in brief sentences.

veil	reindeer	bleach	strawberries	reign
veins	shield	break	automobile	brief
dread	dignified	fear	measured	unified
hear	preach	ready	breakfast	field

1. ______________________________

2. ______________________________

3. ______________________________

4. ______________________________

5. ______________________________

6. ______________________________

7. ______________________________

8. ______________________________

9. ______________________________

10. ______________________________

Lesson 45 - oo Sounds

Rule: The double vowels **oo** usually make the sound you hear in **soon**. The letters **oo** also make the sound you hear in **took**.

DIRECTIONS: Read aloud the sentences below. Underline the words containing **oo**.

1. Jesus and His apostles ate the Last Supper in the Upper Room.
2. The moon was full last night.
3. My dog, Snoopy, is always looking for Dad's tool box.
4. If you took something that was not yours, you must return it.
5. The rooster swooped down on the red wooden wagon.
6. He bought a balloon at the circus.
7. The Bible is called the Good Book.
8. Did you put the spoons away?
9. He put his new boots on the porch.
10. If you look, you can see the red roof tiles.
11. He shook his raincoat and put it on the hook.
12. The children loved to toot the party horns.

DIRECTIONS: Write the **oo** words above in the correct column below.

oo as in **boot**		**oo** as in **book**
______________	______________	______________
______________	______________	______________
______________	______________	______________
______________	______________	______________
______________	______________	______________
______________		______________
		______________
		______________

Lesson 46 - oo Sounds

Rule: The letters **oo** can sound like **oo** in **moon**, **oo** in **took**, or short **u** as in **flood**.

DIRECTIONS: Read the sentences aloud. Put a circle around the words that contain the letters **oo**.

1. St. Catherine of Siena built a chapel in her room.
2. Christ sweat blood in the Garden of Gethsemane.
3. A turnip is the edible root of a plant.
4. The cruel soldiers hammered a single nail in each foot of Jesus.
5. Besides thunder and lightning, the earth shook when Christ died on the Cross.
6. Noah and his family were saved in the Great Flood because he obeyed God and built an ark.
7. St. Helena found the wooden Cross, the true Cross on which Christ was crucified.
8. It is foolish to deny the existence of God when all creation proclaims His glory.
9. Judas took the money for himself.
10. "Don't be sad and gloomy," the father told his children.
11. Jesus loves His Church as a bridegroom loves his bride.
12. Little King, Infant of Prague, we all trust in Thy goodness!

DIRECTIONS: Place each **oo** word above in the proper column below.

oo as in **moon**	**oo** as in **look**	**oo** as in **flood**
________	________	________
________	________	________
________	________	
________	________	
________	________	

Lesson 47 - ui Sounds

Rule: The letters **ui** may have an **oo** sound as in **fruit**, or a short **i** sound as in **build**.

Letters	Word	Sound
ui	fruit	oo
ui	build	i

DIRECTIONS: Read each sentence aloud and underline the words with the **ui** in them. Then circle the sound the word makes.

1. Noah built the Ark according to the instructions of God.

   oo i

2. Eve ate the fruit of the Tree of Knowledge of Good and Evil.

   oo i

3. Have you learned how to make an anniversary quilt?

   oo i

4. The ship was cruising down the Mississippi River.

   oo i

5. In western movies, Roy Rogers often played the guitar while singing songs.

   oo i

6. Did you get a new blue suit for your First Holy Communion?

   oo i

7. When God forgives your sins in Confession, you should no longer feel guilty.

   oo i

8. The blueberry biscuits were made by Father for his small congregation.

   oo i

9. Catholic students should always be in the pursuit of truth.

   oo i

10. Can you name the twelve fruits of the Holy Spirit?

    oo i

11. "There are more vitamins in juice than in that soda pop, children!"

    oo i

12. "Bruised, derided, cursed, defiled, she beheld her Tender Child, all with bloody scourges rent" (Stabat Mater).

    oo i

Lesson 48 - ui Sounds

Rule: The letters **ui** may have an **oo** sound as in **fruit**, or a short **i** sound as in **build**.

DIRECTIONS: Read each sentence aloud. Complete the word(s) in each sentence with **ui**. Then list the words under the correct sound to the right.

1. The new navy cr________ser was in the harbor.
2. The peach was very j________cy.
3. John, the architect, designed the new b________lding.
4. The martyr was br________sed from the deadly beating.
5. It is not s________table behavior to come late to Mass.
6. Grandmother taught the girls how to make q______lts.
7. Jose bought a new g________tar.
8. The loud music was a n________sance.
9. The jury pronounced the prisoner "Not g ______lty."
10. Did you like the blueberry bisc________ts?
11. The police car was in purs________t of the criminal.
12. I like j________cy fr________t.

ui as in **build**

____

____

____

____

____

ui as in **fruit**

____

____

____

____

____

____

____

____

DIRECTIONS: Answer the questions with the words above.

1. What do we call discolored skin? ________________
2. What do we call an old-fashioned bed cover? ________________
3. What is the word for a musical instrument? ________________
4. What do we call a fast chase? ________________
5. What is the opposite word for innocent? ________________

Lesson 49 - Review

DIRECTIONS: Read aloud the words in the list below. Complete the unfinished sentences by writing a word from the list.

cruised	build	took	good	foolish	nuisance
flooded	soon	quilts	fruits	flood	food

Noah was a ______________________ man. He lived in a time when evil was all around him. However, he and his family obeyed God's laws. Most of his neighbors believed that obeying the True God was a ______________________. They didn't want to be disturbed with rules. God was angry with the evil people. He was going to punish them. However, He did not want to punish Noah and his family.

God told Noah to ______________________ an ark. Noah's neighbors thought he was a ______________________ man. He did not care. When the ark was almost finished, Noah ______________________ two of each kind of animal on board. He brought vegetables and ______________________ on board. Then his family went on board and closed up the ark.

The people outside laughed. ______________________ it began to rain. It rained and rained and rained. The earth was ______________________. Everyone on the earth drowned except Noah and his family. The ark ______________________ on top of the water. Inside, the family ate the ______________________ they had stored. They slept under ______________________ they had made for the time in the ark. After forty-seven days, Noah sent forth a dove out of the ark. It came back with a bough of an olive tree in its mouth. When they opened up the covering of the ark, they were on top of a mountain. Noah and his family gave thanks to God for being saved. God promised never again to destroy the world by a ______________________.

Lesson 50 - Review

DIRECTIONS: Read the following words. Then write original sentences using a word with the pair of letters as indicated.

veil	blood	chief	teach	shadow	toast
built	moon	field	break	survey	float
fruit	flood	tried	reach	convey	snow
tie	wood	quilt	steak	cruise	deign

1. ui ______________________________
____
2. oo ______________________________
____
3. ie ______________________________
____
4. ea ______________________________
____
5. ei ______________________________
____
6. ow ______________________________
____
7. oo ______________________________
____
8. oa ______________________________
____
9. ie ______________________________
____
10. ea ______________________________
____

Lesson 51 - the oi & oy Sound

Rule: The letters **oi** and **oy** make the same sound, as in **oil** and **toy**.

DIRECTIONS: Read aloud the list of words below. Underline the **oi** words and circle the **oy** words. Then read aloud and complete the sentences using a word from the list.

soil	joy	royalty	poison	foil	moisture
coin	toys	rejoice	annoy	toil	enjoyed
boy	coin	moist	recoil	Oil	cowboy

1. Do not ______________________ your little brother, Pomeroy!
2. Put the ______________________ in the soda machine to get an orange drink.
3. The ______________________ is marked with skull and crossbones because it is deadly.
4. The ______________________ rides a horse and tends the cattle.
5. All the children ______________________ the movie.
6. The condensation made your clothes ______________________.
7. The farmer will till the ______________________ before he plants his crop.
8. Holy ______________________ , blessed by the bishop on Holy Thursday, is used in Baptism, Confirmation, Holy Orders and Anointing of the Sick.
9. The orphans received ______________________ for Christmas.
10. When presented with a ______________________, Christ said, "Render to Caesar the things that are Caesar's, and to God the things that are God's."
11. While we should ______________________ from sin, we should always love the sinner.
12. Some seed fell upon a rock, and as soon as it sprung up, it withered because it had no ______________________.
13. Be glad and ______________________, for your reward is very great in Heaven.

DIRECTIONS: Write the correct words for descriptions below.

royal   foil   joy   toy

1. Something used for play by children ______________________
2. Paper-thin aluminum to keep food fresh ______________________

Lesson 52 - the oi & oy Sound

DIRECTIONS: Read the words aloud. Underline the **oi** words and circle the **oy** words. Write the words in the list to complete the sentences below as you read them aloud.

avoided	destroy	voyages	appoint	boil	employer
recoiled	convoy	turmoil	moist	enjoy	disappointment

1. Columbus made his ______________________ to discover India.
2. Pride, greed, and envy cause ______________________ among people.
3. Sin should be ______________________ at all cost.
4. Be careful not to ______________________ the property of others.
5. The ships traveled in ______________________to the sea battle.
6. Her ______________________ said she would be promoted.
7. It was a great______________________ when the church was closed.
8. The horse ______________________ at the sight of the snake.

DIRECTIONS: Write the word from the list above next to the proper definition below.

1. ______________________ a group of ships that travel together
2. ______________________ to ruin
3. ______________________ stepped back in fear
4. ______________________ someone who gives others jobs
5. ______________________ trips
6. ______________________ a failure to satisfy the hope or desire of someone
7. ______________________ evaded
8. ______________________ disturbance

Lesson 53 - the ew Sound

Rule: The sound of **ew** is pronounced as in **new**.

DIRECTIONS: In the list below, read each word aloud. Then read the sentences aloud. Write the words to complete the sentences below.

blew	flew	pewter	new	jewelry	news
few	pew	mildew	renew	crew	stew
screw	threw	preview	brew	shrewd	chew
mew	dew	nephew	drew	knew	newspaper

1. Did you ______________________ your pledge to the parish appeal?
2. The bird ______________________ over the church steeple.
3. The ______________________ announced the appointment of the new bishop.
4. Very ______________________ people miss Mass in St. John's parish.
5. His ______________________ came to the family party.
6. Is that a ______________________ dress?
7. The ruby necklace is a fine piece of ______________________.
8. You should genuflect before you go into the ______________________ in church.
9. The candlesticks were made of ______________________.
10. There was ______________________ all over the walls in the damp basement.

DIRECTIONS: Write the **ew** words from the list above in alphabetical order.

______________	______________	______________
______________	______________	______________
______________	______________	______________
______________	______________	______________
______________	______________	______________
______________	______________	______________
______________	______________	______________
______________	______________	______________

Lesson 54 - the ou & ow Sound

Rule: The letters **ou** and **ow** often make the same sound.

Example: p**ou**nd **ou**tside s**ou**nd t**ow**n d**ow**n

DIRECTIONS: Say the words below. Then use the words to complete the following sentences.

drowsy	mouth	Mountains	flower
ground	town	foundation	sour
down	brow	powerful	rowdy
pound	cow	doubtful	flour
counter	slouch		

1. The Easter lily is a beautiful ______________________.
2. The sleepy man was very______________________.
3. The truth of the Resurrection is the ______________________ of our Faith.
4. Buy a______________________ of hamburger for supper.
5. The Rocky ______________________ are beautiful in the fall.
6. Thomas was ______________________ of Christ's Resurrection.
7. Prayer is more ______________________ than anyone knows.
8. The ______________________ passed new traffic laws.
9. Do not ______________________ in your seats, children.
10. The ______________________ jumped over the moon.
11. Jesus told a story about planting seeds in the ______________________.
12. Mother put the plates on the ______________________ in the kitchen.
13. There was a ______________________ crowd at the band concert.
14. The boys jumped up and ______________________when they saw the pope in St. Louis.
15. There were lines in the old man's ______________________.
16. It is not what goes into the mouth of a man which defiles him, but what comes out of his ______________________.

DIRECTIONS: Put the list words in alphabetical order.

____
____
____
____
____
____
____
____
____
____
____
____
____
____
____
____
____
____
____

Lesson 55 - the ou & ow Sound

DIRECTIONS: Circle the words that make the **ou/ow** sound in the puzzle below. Then list them on the lines below.

```
G T O W N F L O W E R Y
J M W N C O U N T E R P
S O C M O U N T A I N O
L U B Z W N R O W D Y W
O T G K F D R O W S Y E
U H R A H A Q T P L B R
O D O U B T F Y O O L F
H O U J L I R V U B T H
P W N B R O W X N C H L
R N D N P N S W D H J C
```

_______________ _______________ _______________

_______________ _______________ _______________

_______________ _______________ _______________

_______________ _______________ _______________

_______________ _______________ _______________

_______________ _______________

DIRECTIONS: Use words from the list above to answer the following questions.

1. What is a very high hill called? _______________
2. Your tongue and teeth are located in what? _______________
3. What animal would you find on a farm? _______________
4. What is a unit for measuring weight? _______________
5. What is a rose? _______________
6. What is the opposite of up? _______________
7. What word means noisy? _______________
8. What is another word for *earth*? _______________

Lesson 56 - Syllables

Rule: Words can be divided into syllables. Each syllable has at least one vowel. Vowels are **a**, **e**, **i**, **o**, **u**, and sometimes **y** (when **y** has the ē or ī sound.)

DIRECTIONS: Read the following words aloud and then divide the words into syllables. Use your dictionary to check your answers if necessary.

Word	Syllables	Word	Syllables
laundry	**laun | dry**	pillow	____________
appliance	____________	balloon	____________
sprawling	____________	suitcase	____________
field	____________	automobile	____________
daylight	____________	building	____________
believed	____________	deceived	____________
feign	____________	citrus	____________
spoonful	____________	speedily	____________
repeat	____________	taunt	____________
moonlight	____________	lawn	____________
abstain	____________	woodwinds	____________
lied	____________	floated	____________
lowered	____________	understanding	____________
unlikely	____________	passengers	____________
motel	____________	lower	____________
hopeless	____________	conveyed	____________
mountain	____________	lawbreaker	____________
applied	____________	mountainous	____________
recede	____________	tourist	____________
crawl	____________	waterproofing	____________
disclaimer	____________	stowaway	____________

Lesson 57 - Review

DIRECTIONS: Read the story below aloud. Complete the unfinished words by filling in **oi**, **oy**, **ew**, **ou**, or **ow**.

Fatima is a village 70 miles ________tside Lisbon, Portugal. It is a small t________n with numer________s little houses hidden away in the m________ntains. In one little hamlet, kn________n as Aljustrel, and the surr________nding hills, a miracle occurred.

A few children, Lucia, Jacinta, and Francisco, were playing in the fields of Fatima in May of 1917. At lunch, they stopped to recite the rosary. A little cl________d hovered over an oak tree in the valley. The cl________d appeared as an ________tline of a moon. The children c________ld not understand this. They realized it was an angel. The angel came forward and led the children in prayer. This was the first of several visits from a Guardian Angel. The children were frightened but joy________s.

The next visitor w________ld be Mary, the Mother of God. She w________ld appear to Lucia, Jacinta, and Francisco. ________r Lady appeared to them once a month from May 13, 1917, to October 13, 1917. The vision br________ght many people to the village. It ann________ed the government officials. Their tempers were b________ling over in August when they arrested the children. ________r Lady did not appear because the children were in jail. However, local officials did not f________l ________r Lady's appearances.

Mary had promised a miracle in October. Many gr________ps came from all over Portugal. They kn________ Mary's message was to pray the rosary, to go to Mass and Confession (on First Saturdays especially), and to do penance. The pilgrims walked for miles in the rain. They prayed the rosary. The cr________d grew larger.

Suddenly, the rain stopped. The children saw Mary appear dressed in sn________ white garments. The children also had visions of ________r Lord, St. Joseph, and then Mary as ________r Lady of Sorr________s. The sun seemed to dance joy________sly in the sky. Suddenly, the sun fell t________ard the earth. This was the miracle Mary had promised. People fell on their knees on the muddy gr________nd. They believed the children. N________there is a Basilica on the spot where Mary appeared to the children of Fatima.

Lesson 58 - Review

DIRECTIONS: Read the Bible selection aloud.

Now when a very great crowd was gathering together and men from every town were hastening to Him, He said in a parable: "The sower went out to sow his seed. And as he sowed, some seed fell by the wayside and was trodden under foot, and the birds of the air ate it up. And other seed fell upon the rock, and as soon as it had sprung up, it withered away, because it had no moisture. And other seed fell among the thorns, and the thorns sprang up with it and choked it. And other seed fell upon good ground, and sprang up and yielded fruit a hundredfold." As He said these things, He cried out, "He who has ears to hear, let him hear!"

But his disciples then began to ask Him what this parable meant. He said to them, "To you it is given to know the mystery of the Kingdom of God, but to the rest in parables, that 'Seeing they may not see, and hearing they may not understand.'

"Now the parable is this: the seed is the word of God. And those by the wayside are they who have heard; then the devil comes and takes away the word from their heart, that they may not believe and be saved. Now those upon the rock are they who, when they have heard, receive the word with joy; and these have no root, but believe for a while, and in time of temptation, fall away. And that which fell among the thorns, these are they who have heard, and as they go their way, are choked by the cares and riches and pleasures of life, and their fruit does not ripen. Those upon good ground, these are they who, with a right and good heart, having heard the word, hold it fast, and bear fruit in patience."

Lesson 59 - Prefixes & Suffixes

Rule: A root is the most basic word part. It is the part of the word which contains the basic meaning of the word.

A prefix is a word part that is added *before* a root.

A suffix is a word part that is added *after* the root.

Root	**Prefix**	**Suffix**	**Word**
appear	dis	ed	disappeared
kind	un	ly	unkindly

Some common prefixes are:

un-	con-
re-	sub-
in-	pro-
dis-	im-

Some common suffixes are:

-ly	-ful
-tion	-ness
-ed	-er
-or	-est

DIRECTIONS: Circle the prefix or suffix in the words below. Then write the words in the appropriate column below.

happiness	unhappy	remind	worked	inside	impractical
disapprove	collector	reader	hotter	propel	inexpensive
darkness	biggest	harmful	redo	kindly	disadvantage
	collection	replace	unclear	merciful	

Words with Prefixes	Words with Suffixes
________________	________________
________________	________________
________________	________________
________________	________________
________________	________________
________________	________________
________________	________________
________________	________________
________________	________________
________________	________________
________________	________________

Lesson 60 - Prefixes: dis & un

Rule: A prefix is a word part added in front of a root which changes its meaning. The root is the basic word part. We can find new words by adding a prefix.

The prefixes **dis** and **un** convey **negative** or **opposite** meaning.

DIRECTIONS: Read the words below aloud and circle the prefix in each.

disembark	disclaim	discord	displace	disapprove
unpleasant	unlawful	unhappy	dispel	unemployed
unbeatable	uneasy	distract	unclear	unsuccessful
discourage	disturb	discharge	unable	unwholesome

DIRECTIONS: Use the dictionary to write a definition for the following words.

1. disclaim ______________________________

2. disembark ______________________________

3. discord ______________________________

4. dispel ______________________________

5. discharge ______________________________

6. uneasy ______________________________

7. unwholesome ______________________________

8. unable ______________________________

Lesson 61 - Prefixes: ir, in, im, un, & dis

Rule: A prefix is a word part that is added before a root, the basic word part.

The following prefixes convey **negative** meaning or **opposite** meaning: **ir**, **in**, **im**, **un**, and **dis**.

Word	Definition	Word	Definition
infidel	not faithful	discontented	not content
impatient	not patient	unfriendly	not friendly
irreverent	not reverent		

DIRECTIONS: Read the following sentences aloud. Underline the word in each sentence that has a prefix meaning <u>not</u>.

1. Some Franciscan orders were called "discalced" because they did not wear shoes.
2. There is an irregularity in our zoning laws, the mayor said.
3. The pain the martyr suffered seemed unbearable to the crowd.
4. There was an indefinite delay in the arrival of the bishop's plane.
5. The Jews use unleavened bread at Passover.
6. Our faith is an irreplaceable gift from God.
7. Older people have a dispensation and may eat between meals during Lent.
8. Our pastor disapproves of wearing shorts at Mass.
9. The streets of New York City are unsafe at night.
10. It is improper to speak loudly in church.
11. The rain was infrequent last summer, and farmers lost their crops.
12. Sinners are unhappy people inside themselves.

DIRECTIONS: Make a new word by adding a prefix from above.

_______happy _______frequent _______polite

_______pleased _______regular _______belief

DIRECTIONS: Write below some words from your reader which have a prefix **ir, in**, **im**, **un**, or **dis**.

_______________ _______________ _______________

_______________ _______________ _______________

_______________ _______________ _______________

_______________ _______________ _______________

_______________ _______________ _______________

_______________ _______________ _______________

Lesson 62 - Prefixes: ir, in, im, un, & dis

Rule: A prefix is a word part that is added before a root, the basic word part.

DIRECTIONS: Write a word from the list below that correctly completes each unfinished sentence below. Read the words and sentences aloud as you go.

disbelief	unearthly	irrefutable	inability	displaced	unlike
irrational	intolerant	impossible	impurity	irreparable	inactive

1. The twins were not identical. They were very ______________________ each other.
2. The lights above were very strange. They had an ______________________ quality about them.
3. Mary did not believe what John told her. He could not understand her ______________________.
4. The men could not do their job. It was an ______________________ task.
5. The TV show was full of bad language. We turned the TV off because of the ______________________ of the show.
6. All the evidence was there to convict the criminal. It was ______________________ evidence.
7. A madman behaves without reason. His actions are ______________________.
8. The old member of the Legion of Mary no longer comes to meetings. He is an ______________________ member.
9. The people who fled Germany during World War II lived away from their normal homes. They were called ______________________ persons.
10. The boys were mean to people who were different. The boys were ______________________.
11. The newspaper article told lies about the man. It did______________________ damage to the man's reputation.
12. The teenager did not have the qualifications for the job. Therefore, he was not hired because of his ______________________ to do the work.

DIRECTIONS: Write the list words in alphabetical order below.

______________________	______________________
______________________	______________________
______________________	______________________
______________________	______________________
______________________	______________________
______________________	______________________

Lesson 63 - Prefixes: in & en

Rule: A prefix is a word part that is added before a root, the basic word part.

The prefixes **in** and **en** are sometimes used to mean **cause to be**, or **make**.

Prefix	Word	Definition
en	encounter	to cause people to meet
in	intone	to make a prolonged chant

DIRECTIONS: Choose the word that best completes each sentence.

1. Columbus ______________________ many hardships to discover America.
   intoned endured insult
2. The pope is ______________________ when teaching about Faith and morals.
   enraptured inscribed infallible
3. The cloistered nuns live by the rule of ______________________, by which they choose to remain away from the outside world.
   enclosure ingrained encrusted
4. God bestows ______________________ blessings on those who live according to His laws.
   incense enfolded innumerable
5. The friars ______________________ Gregorian Chant as they walked to the chapel for Vespers.
   enlarge intoned intellect
6. Mary ______________________ her donation to her parish last year.
   ensured inflated increased
7. The hunter ______________________ the wild jaguar in his net.
   ensnared informed enframed
8. The monks ______________________ the Book of Kells in beautiful colors.
   enmeshed inscribed entangled

DIRECTIONS: Complete the rule.

The prefixes **in** or **en** can mean ______________________ or ______________________.

DIRECTIONS: Write some words from your reader that start with **in** or **en**.

______________________ ______________________

______________________ ______________________

______________________ ______________________

______________________ ______________________

Lesson 64 - Prefixes: in & en

A prefix is a word part that is added before a root, the basic word part.

DIRECTIONS: Match the word in the first column with the definition. Write the correct word in front of each definition. Use your dictionary if you do not know the word.

infuse	1. ____________________	to move by divine influence
enrobe	2. ____________________	to follow as a consequence
inspire	3. ____________________	to dress in long garments
enchain	4. ____________________	to live in a place
indulgence	5. ____________________	to make larger
increase	6. ____________________	remission of punishment due to sin
ensue	7. ____________________	to put in a cage
enwrap	8. ____________________	to instill, to put into
inhabit	9. ____________________	to put in a wrapping
encage	10. ____________________	to put in place with a chain

DIRECTIONS: Use a form of one of the list words above to answer the following questions.

1. What would you do with a lion? ______________________________

2. What would you do with a gift package? __________________________

3. What do we believe Matthew, Mark, Luke, and John were when they wrote the Bible?

4. Besides being crowned, what is done to a king at his coronation? ____________

5. What do we receive if we say the Rosary before the Blessed Sacrament? __________

6. What does the pastor ask you to do with your donations when the parish needs money?

7. How do we receive the virtues that accompany sanctifying grace? ______________

Lesson 65 - Prefixes: mis & mal

Rule: A prefix is a word part that is added before a root word, the basic word part.

Prefixes **mis** and **mal** usually mean **bad** or **badly**.

Prefix	Word	Definition
mis	misinformed	informed badly
mal	malfunction	not functioning well

DIRECTIONS: Read each word aloud. Then write the correct word for the sentences.

malformed	mismatched	mislead	misuse	misbehave	malfunctioned
malpractice	misplaced	mistrust	mislaid	misguided	misinterpreted

1. Jesus cured many who were lame because their feet were ____________________ at birth.
2. My computer does not work. It has ____________________ for two days.
3. The road signs were turned around. They will ____________________ people who drive by.
4. Joan could not remember where she placed her glasses. She had ____________________ them.
5. Peter gave the people the wrong directions. He ____________________ them.
6. Dave wore one red sock and one blue sock. The socks were ____________________.
7. The man lied often. People had only ____________________ for him.
8. The doctor used the wrong drug on his patient. As a result, the patient filed a ____________________ lawsuit against the doctor.
9. Take care of your bicycle. Do not ____________________ it and you will have it for years.
10. Mother told the boys not to ____________________ while she is gone.
11. Aunt Ruth ____________________ her purse when she was at the store.
12. Many non-Catholics have ____________________ the words of Jesus to Peter, "Upon this rock, I will build My Church."

Lesson 66 - Prefixes: mis & mal

A prefix is a word part that is added before a root, the basic word part.

DIRECTIONS: Read the word list aloud. Read the sentences aloud. Write one of the list words to replace words in each sentence. Write out the new sentence. Use the dictionary if you do not know the meaning of a word.

mislead	misquote	mistreated	maladjusted
mistrial	misfortune	malcontent	malnourishment
misused	misnamed	malediction	misconduct

1. The child was given the wrong name at the hospital.

   ____

2. The devil worked to trick Eve into sin.

   ____

3. Often newspapers do not correctly quote people.

   ____

4. If appliances are not used correctly, they could cause a fire.

   ____

5. The children in the orphanage suffered from lack of food.

   ____

6. The author of *Black Beauty* showed that some horses are not treated well.

   ____

7. The judge declared the accused man had a bad trial.

   ____

8. Babies who are not given affection often become lonely and unhappy later in life.

   ____

9. The soldier was disciplined by his captain for bad behavior.

   ____

10. The young boy had a great deal of bad luck.

   ____

Lesson 67 - Prefixes: un, dis, ir, im, in, en, mis, & mal

A prefix is a word part that is added to a root, the basic word part.

DIRECTIONS: Read the story aloud. Circle the words that begin with the prefixes: **un**, **dis**, **ir**, **im**, **in**, **en**, **mis,** and **mal**.

An Unlikely Saint

Edmund Campion was the son of a bookseller. His parents were indifferent Catholics who left the Church. They had the misfortune of living in Elizabethan England. It would have been impractical to stay in the Roman Catholic Church. Catholics were distrusted and maltreated because they disagreed with the Church of England.

When Edmund was born, it would have been impossible for anyone to believe he would one day become a Catholic saint. Edmund was an extremely bright boy. He had the misfortune of being sent to study at Oxford. Here it was not irregular for people not only to disbelieve, but also to become entangled in groups that actively persecuted Catholics. Edmund became a deacon in the Anglican church. He even took the Royal Supremacy Oath.

However, God would work in His own way. Edmund started reading. As he discovered the true history of England and the misunderstood writings of the Church Fathers, he realized that the Roman Catholic Church was not irreverent and mistaken, but it was the one true Church. Edmund started preaching increasingly against the English heresy. He was forced to flee England. He disembarked at France. He went to Douai and then to Rome to study, and later became a Jesuit priest.

Returning to England quietly, as priests were unwelcome there, Edmund offered Mass in people's homes, wrote dissertations, and administered the sacraments. All of these acts endangered his life. After the publication of *Decem Rationes*, he was hunted down by the government. He was betrayed by friends. He was enchained and finally imprisoned in the Tower of London. On December 1, 1581, he was hanged for his refusal to deny the Catholic Faith. He was canonized with the English martyrs in 1970.

Lesson 68 - Prefix Review

DIRECTIONS: Circle the words with prefixes and write them on the line.

1. Edmund Campion's parents left the Church because they were indifferent Catholics.

   ____

2. The Campions lived in Elizabethan England where Catholics were mistreated and persecuted.

   ____

3. Edmund was forced to take the Royal Supremacy Oath because the Protestant government was intolerant of Catholics.

   ____

4. Edmund did not misuse his time as he struggled to find God's truths.

   ____

5. Once he learned his education was incorrect, Edmund converted and became a Catholic priest.

   ____

6. Jesuits were unwelcome in England because they disagreed with the Anglican church's teachings.

   ____

7. English Catholics were in such need of priests, Edmund was unafraid to go back to England.

   ____

8. Edmund would not mislead his people.

   ____

9. He was inspired to preach the truths of the Roman Catholic Church.

   ____

10. He was imprisoned and hanged.

    ____

11. Those who were informed realized the injustice.

    ____

Lesson 69 - Prefixes: pre & pro

A prefix is a word part that is added before a root, basic word part.

Rule: The prefixes **pre** and **pro** usually mean **before**. The prefix **pro** can also mean **for** or **forward**.

Prefix	Word	Definition
pro	pro-life	for life
pro	promote	to go forward, often in a job
pre	presanctified	consecrated or transubstantiated earlier

DIRECTIONS: Read the word list aloud. Use your dictionary for words you do not know. Write a list word to fit each definition.

preface	preview	propose	promote
prospective	propel	pro-life	prepay
preheat	proceed	prevent	precaution

1. ____________________ to see before presented publicly
2. ____________________ to drive forward
3. ____________________ to make a suggestion
4. ____________________ likely or expected to happen
5. ____________________ to stop before it happens
6. ____________________ a section that introduces a book
7. ____________________ care before acting
8. ____________________ to be for life
9. ____________________ to move ahead
10. ____________________ to raise to a more important rank
11. ____________________ to heat before
12. ____________________ to pay before

DIRECTIONS: Write a sentence for two of the list words above.

1. ____

____

2. ____

____

Lesson 70 - Prefixes: pre & pro

A prefix is a word part added before a root, the basic word part.

DIRECTIONS: Read the definitions below. Read the list of words on the right aloud. Put the letter of the word in front of the correct definition.

	Definition	Word
____	1. an act to prevent an accident	a. propose
____	2. to make a suggestion	b. preface
____	3. to force ahead	c. prepay
____	4. a section that introduces a book	d. promotion
____	5. to go forward with a planned act	e. presumption
____	6. to pay ahead	f. presanctified
____	7. a move up, as in a job	g. precaution
____	8. not to allow an act	h. proceed
____	9. consecrated earlier	i. propel
____	10. unfounded expectation	j. prohibit

DIRECTIONS: Write a sentence for each word: proclaim, prepared, protest, prolong, preoccupy, precook, and predict.

1. ____
____

2. ____
____

3. ____
____

4. ____
____

5. ____
____

6. ____
____

7. ____
____

Lesson 71 - Prefixes: re & ex

A prefix is a word part that is added before a root, the basic word part.

Rule: The prefix **re** means **over again**. The prefix **ex** means **out of** or **from**.

Prefix	Word	Definition
re	replace	to put back again
re	reverse	to turn back again
ex	explosion	to blow out from
ex	extreme	out of the usual

DIRECTIONS: Read the sentences aloud. Write the correct word in the sentences. Use the dictionary if you do not know the meaning.

exempt	excuses	reform	reverse	exodus	excommunicated
reprinted	exercise	return	export	expect	examination
Exposition	response	recall	extend	reassured	

1. The student ______________________ the magazine article for her friends to read.
2. The ladies went to ______________________ class at the gym every morning.
3. After confession, you must try to ______________________ your life.
4. The company agreed to ______________________ the payments for six months.
5. Did you take your last ______________________ for the school year?
6. If you put a car in ______________________, it will go backwards.
7. King Henry VIII was ______________________ from the Catholic Church.
8. Mom said I was ______________________ from my chores because I am sick.
9. On First Fridays, our parish has ______________________ of the Blessed Sacrament.
10. The old lady could not ______________________ events from long ago.
11. After only one leper came back to give thanks, Jesus said, "There is no one found to ______________________ and give glory to God but this stranger."
12. Jesus told a story of a man who invited his friends to a great supper, but at the hour of the banquet, they began to make ______________________ for not coming.
13. Mary's ______________________ to the Archangel Gabriel was, "Be it done to me according to thy word."
14. The doctor __________________ Mom that the sickness was not contagious.

Lesson 72 - Prefixes: re & ex

A prefix is a word part that is added before a root, the basic word part.

DIRECTIONS: Fill in the blanks with the correct prefix: **re** or **ex**.

1. The architect had to _________cavate the ruins of the early Christian city.
2. Remember to _________cap the soda so it does not go flat.
3. The family had to _________build the house after the fire.
4. Did you see the Vatican _________hibit at the Smithsonian Museum?
5. Since you failed the test, you must _________do the work.
6. The _________plosion at the World Trade Center destroyed the hotel and the garage.
7. Women were allowed to _________join their religious orders after the French Revolution.
8. The pope _________communicated Martin Luther.
9. To improve your composition, _________read it and write it over again.
10. Members who do not obey the rules of the Knights of Columbus can be ______pelled.

DIRECTIONS: Write in the appropriate column below the words you have corrected above. Look in the dictionary for the definitions.

ex	re
________________________	________________________
________________________	________________________
________________________	________________________
________________________	________________________
________________________	________________________

DIRECTIONS: Fill in the following sentences using words having the **ex** prefix.

1. A Catholic who is ______________________ may not receive the Sacraments.
2. Before confessing your sins, you must ______________________ your conscience.

Lesson 73 - Prefixes: fore & post

A prefix is a word part that is added before a root, the basic word part.

Rule: The prefix **post** means **after**. The prefix **fore** means **in front of** or **before**.

Prefix	Word	Root	Definition
fore	forehead	head	the front of the head
post	postcommunion	communion	after communion

DIRECTIONS: Read the word list aloud. Write the word, the prefix, and the root of each word. Write the definition from the dictionary.

foresee	forecast	postscript	forefather
postwar	postdate	forearm	forethought
foretold	foresight	foretaste	postgraduate

Word	Prefix	Root	Definition
(ex.) postpone	post	pone	to put off until later

Lesson 74 - Prefixes: fore & post

A prefix is word part that is added before a root, the basic word part.

DIRECTIONS: Using a dictionary, write a definition for the following words.

1. foreground ______________________________
2. forefront ______________________________
3. foreshadow ______________________________
4. forefather ______________________________
5. forestall ______________________________
6. postpone ______________________________
7. posterity ______________________________
8. postscript ______________________________
9. forecast ______________________________
10. forenoon ______________________________

Lesson 75 - Prefixes: fore, ex, & re

DIRECTIONS: Read the following words aloud. Match each word in the list with the proper definition below and write the selected word beside each definition.

foremost	recapture	exhort	exceed
forecast	excursion	recall	rebirth
foregone	foresight	rebuke	exclaim
excess	forearm	rebook	

1. ______________________ the act of retaking or recovering
2. ______________________ a short journey; an outing
3. ______________________ knowing the significance of something before it happens
4. ______________________ having more than what is normal or sufficient
5. ______________________ to change a performance or reservation
6. ______________________ the first in time or place
7. ______________________ to criticize severely
8. ______________________ to cry out suddenly
9. ______________________ to ask or order to return
10. ______________________ to be greater; surpass
11. ______________________ having gone before; previous
12. ______________________ a second or new birth
13. ______________________ to estimate or calculate in advance
14. ______________________ to make urgent appeal
15. ______________________ the part of the arm between the wrist and the elbow

DIRECTIONS: Select two **ex** words, two **fore** words, and two **re** words from the list above. Write each of the selected words in a sentence.

1. ____
2. ____
3. ____
4. ____
5. ____
6. ____

Lesson 76 - Prefixes: pre & pro

A prefix is a word part that is added before a root, the basic word part.

Rule: **Pre** and **pro** are prefixes that usually mean **before**. **Pro** can also mean **forward**.

DIRECTIONS: Read the following words aloud. Write the correct word on the line beside the correct definition.

preamble	precise	preclude	predict	proceed	prepare
proclaim	profound	propose	provoke	procedure	prolong
precede	precept	precut	premiere	promotion	projection
produce	program	protest	provide	preconceive	premature

1. ____________________ a schedule of events before they happen
2. ____________________ to come, exist or occur before
3. ____________________ to furnish or supply before they are needed
4. ____________________ the first public performance coming before the others
5. ____________________ clearly expressed
6. ____________________ deep, far-reaching, penetrating in insight
7. ____________________ to make impossible; to close off before something happens
8. ____________________ to stir beforehand to action or feeling
9. ____________________ an introduction to a formal document
10. ____________________ cut in size or shape before
11. ____________________ to object to something before it happens, usually
12. ____________________ to make known in advance before it happens
13. ____________________ to put forward for consideration before it happens
14. ____________________ to declare officially and publicly before it happens
15. ____________________ to create or bring forth
16. ____________________ a rule that commands a certain action in the future

DIRECTIONS: Select three **pre** words and three **pro** words from the list above. Use each word in a sentence.

1. ____
2. ____
3. ____
4. ____
5. ____
6. ____

Lesson 77 - Prefix: over

A prefix is word part that is added before a root, the basic word part.

Rule: When the prefix **over** is placed in front of an adjective, it usually means **too much**.

Example: overanxious overabundant overeager

When the prefix **over** is placed in front of a verb, the prefix usually means **too much**.

Example: overwork overdone overspend

DIRECTIONS: Read the following words aloud. Write on the line the word from the list that best completes the sentence.

overworked	overserious	overconfident	overtired	overspent
overexercise	oversweet	overprotective	overripe	overdone
overcrowded	overflowed	overpopulated	overheat	overpriced
overanxious	overweight			

1. A mother cannot be ______________________ of her children when traveling.
2. Dad worked long hours and became ______________________ last week.
3. Because Sally ______________________ at the auction, she had no money for her rent.
4. The store was ______________________ but you could still squeeze through the people.
5. The greedy storeowner ______________________ the goods on his shelves.
6. The mother did much more work than she should have. She was

   ______________________.
7. The river ______________________ during the hurricane.
8. The motorcycle rider was ______________________ and missed the distant goal.
9. The boy became ______________________ about his broken toy.
10. The ______________________ apples were going bad in the bushel baskets.
11. Be careful not to ______________________ or your muscles will hurt!
12. The meat tasted burnt because it was ______________________.
13. The world is not ______________________ but many people live in large congested cities.
14. The 100° temperature in Washington, D.C., caused many cars to

    ______________________.
15. Most Americans believe they are ______________________ and are constantly dieting!

Lesson 78 - Prefix: over

A prefix is a word part added before a root, the basic word part.

DIRECTIONS: Read the sentences aloud. Then write in the correct word to complete each sentence.

1. Because the president's hopes were too high, he was called ____________________.

   optimistic   overoptimistic

2. A storeowner that ________________________ his goods is sinning against the commandment that forbids stealing.

   price   overprices

3. Bishop Athanasius of Alexandria was ______________________ of the Catholic Faith when he preached against heresy.

   protective   overprotective

4. Jane's sister paid $15.00 for the book, but it cost only $13.99. She had made a(n) ______________________ of $1.01.

   payment   overpayment

5. A dog that is ______________________ will become fat.

   overfed   fed

6. The boy did not have much money, so he was careful not to ______________________ at the state fair.

   overspend   spend

7. The grapes were turning brown on the vine because they were _________________.

   overripe   ripe

8. Because God is the Creator of each person, we can never believe that the world is ______________________.

   populated   overpopulated

9. The trim-looking, older gentleman was healthy and fit from ______________________ every day.

   exercising   overexercising

10. The ruins of the old monastery were ______________________ with vegetation and weeds.

    grown   overgrown

Read the words below aloud. Do you know what they mean?

overtalkative	overeager	overstocked	overambitious
overdressed	overtired	overreacted	overbalanced
overstepped	overused	overplayed	overcome

Lesson 79 - Prefixes: co, com, & con

A prefix is a word part added before a root, the basic part of the word.

Rule: The prefixes **co**, **com,** and **con** mean **to work with** or **to join together**.

Prefix	Word	Definition
co	co-consecrators	two priests who consecrate together
com	commission	people who study a topic together
con	concur	to agree together

DIRECTIONS: Read the sentences aloud and write the word that correctly completes each sentence.

1. When boys and girls are taught together, it is called ________________________.

   conserve　　commerce　　co-education

2. The date of her birthday will ________________________ with Easter.

   companion　　conquer　　coincide

3. Was it really a ____________________ that St. Ignatius Loyola met St. Francis Xavier?

   compose　　conserve　　coincidence

4. The Pope ________________________ Easter Mass with the bishops on Easter Sunday.

   commission　　concelebrated　　co-consecrators

5. If we all ________________________, we can repair the altar railing quickly.

   coincide　　consecutive　　cooperate

6. Pizarro and the Spanish conquistadors fought together to ______________________ Peru.

   coincide　　complicate　　conquer

7. Mozart ________________________ the famous opera *Don Giovanni*.

   composed　　consoled　　communicated

8. Nuns never travelled alone; they always had a traveling ________________________.

   companion　　cowriter　　conserve

9. The nuns visited the nursing home to ______________________ the old people.

   common　　console　　coincidence

10. The graduates planned their ________________________ exercise for two weeks.

    consume　　cooperate　　commencement

11. The papal________________________ prepared a report for the pope.

    conserve　　conquer　　commission

12. Daniel, the prophet, predicted seven ________________________ years of famine.

    cooperate　　common　　consecutive

Lesson 80 - Prefixes: co, com, & con

A prefix is a word part added before a root, the basic word part.

Rule: The prefixes **co**, **com**, and **con** mean **to work with** or **to join together**.

DIRECTIONS: Write one of the prefixes in front of the root words below. The complete word should match the definition.

1. __________pose: to write music or poetry (by joining words or notes)
2. __________plete: to finish or make whole (by joining together)
3. __________tagious: easily spread from one to another (by joining people together)
4. __________pany: people grouped together as guests or visitors
5. __________secutive: one thing following another
6. __________panion: synonym for friend (someone together with someone else)
7. __________incide: to go together or fit together
8. __________spiracy: a secret plan (by people who join together)
9. __________celebrate: two who join together to celebrate
10. __________operate: to work together

DIRECTIONS: Write the words above to complete correctly the following sentences.

1. After the forty ______________________ days of rain had stopped, Noah sent out a dove to see if the waters were receding.
2. You need two priests to ____________________ Mass.
3. When people ____________________ in the fight against evil, they obtain better results.
4. Maureen has the ______________________ edition of *Butler's Lives of the Saints.*
5. Pope St. Gregory ______________________ the liturgical music known as Gregorian Chant.
6. Tuberculosis is a dangerous ______________________ disease.
7. Our family had ______________________ visiting for the weekend.
8. Peter was Christ's constant ______________________ during His public life.
9. Many people believe there was a ________________________ behind the attempted assassination of the pope.
10. Some significant historical events ____________________ with important feast days of the Church calendar.

Lesson 81 - Prefixes: sub & mid

A prefix is a word part added before a root, the basic part of the word.

Rule: **Mid** can mean **the middle part. Sub** can mean **below, under,** or **not quite.**

Prefix	Word	Definition
mid	midway	halfway between two points
sub	substandard	below the requirement needed to make something acceptable

DIRECTIONS: Read each word aloud. Write the correct word on the line provided in front of the definition.

submarine	subject	midday	midnight	subside	subdeacon
midstream	subway	midway	midweek	submerge	substandard
midocean	midyear	midair	subtract		

1. ______________________ halfway between the ground and the sky
2. ______________________ to be under someone's authority
3. ______________________ halfway between U.S. and Europe on the Atlantic
4. ______________________ train that travels underground
5. ______________________ halfway through the year
6. ______________________ first step before becoming deacon
7. ______________________ what Wednesday is
8. ______________________ to go underwater
9. ______________________ below an acceptable level
10. ______________________ noon
11. ______________________ ship that travels underwater
12. ______________________ halfway downstream

DIRECTIONS: Write six sentences using words from list above.

1. ____
2. ____
3. ____
4. ____
5. ____
6. ____

Lesson 82 - Prefixes: sub & mid

DIRECTIONS: Write the words from Lesson 81 to fill in the blanks in the sentences below.

1. The Christmas break comes ______________________ in the usual school year.
2. Doctors take Wednesday off because it is a ______________________ break.
3. We should all be ______________________ to Christ the King.
4. It was ______________________ when the soldiers nailed Jesus to the Cross.
5. They had to ______________________ the drill in the water to fix the well pump.
6. The Washington, D.C. ______________________ is crowded after work hours.
7. The ships stopped to refuel ______________________ between New York and Brazil.
8. We leave at eleven on Christmas Eve to attend ______________________ Mass.
9. Hawaii is ______________________ between North America and Asia.
10. The young man prepared with much prayer before becoming a __________________.
11. The ______________________ raised its periscope to spot the enemy destroyer.
12. The mayor said, "No one should have to live in ______________________ housing."

DIRECTIONS: Write a definition and a sentence for each word in the space below.

submarine

Definition: ____

Sentence: ____

subtract

Definition: ____

Sentence: ____

midnight

Definition: ____

Sentence: ____

midweek

Definition: ____

Sentence: ____

Lesson 83 - Prefixes: bi & tri

Rule: The prefix **bi** means **two**. The prefix **tri** means **three**.

Prefix	**Word**	**Definition**
bi	bicycle	cycle with two wheels
tri	triune	three in one

1. biweekly—happening once every two weeks
2. bifocals—eyeglasses with two sections or lenses
3. triduum—three days of special prayer
4. Trinity—Three Persons in One God, the Triune God

DIRECTIONS: Look in the dictionary and write the definitions for the words below.

---

1. bisect ____
____
2. biplane ____
____
3. triangle ____
____
4. tricycle ____
____

DIRECTIONS: Fill in the missing words.

---

1. A bicycle has two ____________________.
2. A bilingual person can speak two ____________________.
3. Biweekly means happening twice a ____________________.
4. A triangle has three ____________________.
5. A tripod has three ____________________.
6. A trident is a spear with three ____________________.

Lesson 84 - Prefixes: bi & tri

DIRECTIONS: Read aloud the list of words below. Write each word next to the proper definition.

bicycle	bilingual	binoculars	bimonthly	bicentennial
triangle	biennial	bicolored	tricolored	tricentennial
triplets	triennial	trimonthly	tricycle	

1.__________________ a figure having three angles.

2.__________________ has two wheels

3.__________________ has three colors

4.__________________ done every two years

5.__________________ done every three months

6.__________________ two hundredth anniversary or celebration

7.__________________ has three wheels

8.__________________ done every three years

9.__________________ three hundredth anniversary or celebration

10.__________________ done every two months

11.__________________ speaks two languages

12.__________________ has two colors

DIRECTIONS: Write below some of the above list words in sentences.

1.____

2.____

3.____

4.____

5.____

6.____

7.____

8.____

9.____

10.____

11.____

12.____

Lesson 85 - Review

DIRECTIONS: This story has words containing the prefixes **over, bi, tri, sub, mid, con, co,** and **com.** Read the story and underline the words that begin with these prefixes.

The Triune God

Since it was revealed by God in the Bible, we know that God is Three Divine Persons in one Divine Nature. We call this the Blessed Trinity. We do not understand this, but we subject our will to the revealed Word of God and we do believe. There is no midground in this belief. We must believe wholeheartedly and completely.

The Father is the First Person of the Blessed Trinity. He created man in His image. The Father made man overseer of all the earth. The animals were all subservient to Adam and Eve. Unfortunately, our first parents cooperated with Satan and brought sin into the world. When God asked what they had done, Adam complained that Eve made him do it. They were, however, bilaterally responsible for the sin of prideful disobedience. God commanded St. Michael the Archangel to drive them from the Garden of Eden. Compassionately, the Father promised to send a Redeemer.

Jesus Christ is the Second Person of the Blessed Trinity. Because of His love for men, Christ subjected Himself to the humbling act of becoming one of us. His concern for our salvation made Him suffer and die for our sins. If we cooperate with the grace He offers us, we will be saved. We should be overwhelmed with gratitude for His sacrifice.

The Holy Spirit is the Third Person of the Blessed Trinity. He is also called the Holy Ghost. When we are in the state of grace, we have God's life within us. Our bodies become temples of the Holy Spirit. The importance of the Holy Spirit cannot be overstated. Through Him flows grace, the life of the soul. When we are baptized, He comes into our souls. At Confirmation, the Holy Spirit comes to us in a special way, and enables us to profess our Faith as strong Christians and soldiers of Jesus Christ.

The Three Persons in the Triune God will give us help whenever we ask. Submission to the will of God and obedience to His law increase grace in us. Only willful, deliberate, serious disobedience, called mortal sin, can drive Him away. We can be consoled by the fact that if we are sorry and go to Confession, if we have true contrition, our sins will be forgiven. We should always try to live in the state of grace.

Lesson 86 - Review

DIRECTIONS: Write the words you underlined in the story in Lesson 85. Write the repeated words only once.

1. ____________ 2. ____________ 3. ____________
4. ____________ 5. ____________ 6. ____________
7. ____________ 8. ____________ 9. ____________
10. ____________ 11. ____________ 12. ____________
13. ____________ 14. ____________ 15. ____________
16. ____________ 17. ____________ 18. ____________
19. ____________ 20. ____________

DIRECTIONS: Answer the following questions by including a word from the list above.

1. What did Adam and Eve do that offended God?

2. What did God reveal in the Bible about Himself?

3. What did God make man over the animals?

4. What did Christ do because of His love for men?

5. How should we feel when we know God forgives those who are sorry for their sins?

6. What were the animals' relationship to Adam and Eve?

7. In which sacrament does the Holy Spirit come to make us soldiers of Jesus Christ?

8. What do we have to do with the grace Christ offers us to be saved?

9. How much gratitude should we have for Christ's suffering and death?

10. In which sacrament do we confess our sins?

Lesson 87 - Roots: pos & pel

Rule: Prefixes and suffixes are added to root words. The root is the base word or basic word part. Prefixes and suffixes alter the meaning of the word.

The root **pos** means **put** or **place**. When combined with a prefix, the root can form words such as compose (put together), expose (place out for viewing), repose (place again), depose (place away from), or deposit (put in a bank).

The root **pel** means **drive** or **force**. When combined with a prefix, the root can form words such as compel (force), expel (drive away), or dispel (drive apart or drive away).

DIRECTIONS: Read the sentences. Write the root that completes the word. Use **pos** or **pel.**

---

1. The monks com_____ed music for every single feast day of the liturgical year.
2. The king decided to ex_____ all thieves and revolutionaries from his kingdom.
3. On First Fridays, our parish has Ex____ition of the Most Blessed Sacrament.
4. St. Martin's love for God com_____led him to help poor people in Lima, Peru.
5. The cruel and foolish general com_____led his soldiers to march in the desert in the blistering heat all day long.
6. There is an ex_____ition of religious art in the parish hall.
7. The homeschool students wrote many excellent com_____itions.
8. When we were children, our parents ex_____ed us to quality classical music.
9. On the first Easter Sunday, Our Lord Jesus Christ dis_____led the darkness of sin and death.
10. The king's loyal soldiers will de_____e the usurper-king.

DIRECTIONS: Write the **pos** and **pel** words from the sentences above.

---

1. ____________________ 2. ____________________ 3. ____________________

4. ____________________ 5. ____________________ 6. ____________________

7. ____________________ 8. ____________________ 9. ____________________

10. ____________________

DIRECTIONS: Choose one of the words from the above exercise and use it in a sentence.

____

____

____

Lesson 88 - Roots: port & ject

Root	Word	Definition
port (carry)	report	to carry a story
ject (throw, force)	eject	to throw off or out

DIRECTIONS: In the sentences below, circle the words with roots **port** or **ject**.

1. The young girl's comportment was very good for her age.
2. Jesus was rejected as the Messiah by the leaders of the Jews.
3. We should ask Jesus to help us feel better if we become dejected.
4. We can hear Mother Angelica on our shortwave portable radio!
5. Only qualified doctors and nurses may give people injections.
6. The porter took our bags on the train when we visited the Vatican.
7. The manufacturer will export most of his products to poor countries.
8. Did the pilot eject from the jet when the cockpit caught fire?

DIRECTIONS: Write the words you circled in the sentences above. Use a dictionary to write the definition next to each word.

	Word	Definition
1.	____________	____________________
2.	____________	____________________
3.	____________	____________________
4.	____________	____________________
5.	____________	____________________
6.	____________	____________________
7.	____________	____________________
8.	____________	____________________

Lesson 89 - Roots: aud & dict

Root	Word	Definition
aud (hear)	audience	a group of listeners
dict (say, tell)	dictate	to speak for someone; to write down

DIRECTIONS: In the following sentences, circle the words with **aud** or **dict** roots.

1. The Major Domo allowed us to enter the Consistory Hall to attend a papal audience.
2. Hitler was a cruel dictator who persecuted and murdered Jews and Catholics.
3. The audio tape of Bishop Sheen helped us prepare for Confession.
4. We use the dictionary to help with phonics lessons.
5. The pianist auditioned with the Julliard School of Music!
6. Will Father use audio-visual material to teach the next Religion lesson?
7. Jesus said no one can predict when the end of the world will come.
8. The judge read the verdict decided by the jury.
9. Dad said we should never contradict our mother.
10. The young nun took dictation from her Mother Superior.

DIRECTIONS: Write below the words you underlined above. Use your dictionary to write the definitions next to the words.

	Word	Definition
1.	____________________	________________________________
2.	____________________	________________________________
3.	____________________	________________________________
4.	____________________	________________________________
5.	____________________	________________________________
6.	____________________	________________________________
7.	____________________	________________________________
8.	____________________	________________________________
9.	____________________	________________________________
10.	____________________	________________________________

Lesson 90 - Roots: duct & duc, scribe & script

Root	**Word**	**Definition**
duct, duc (lead)	educate	lead to the truth
scribe, script (write)	description	a written picture

DIRECTIONS: Circle the words with **duc**, **duct**, **scribe**, or **script** roots in the following sentences.

1. The inscription on the tomb read, "Requiescat in Pace," which means "Rest in Peace."
2. Did Mary introduce you to her brother, Joseph?
3. The conductor waved the lamp to signal that it was safe to start the train.
4. Pontius Pilate insisted that INRI be inscribed on the Cross of Jesus!
5. The police asked the eyewitness for a full description of the car thief.
6. Father Brown did not want to reduce the songs for the Candlemas procession.
7. The pastor asked if we would subscribe to the Catholic newspaper.
8. An educator should be leading students to the truth about God.
9. The higher inventory showed the workers were more productive.
10. Mom was pleased that the girls' conduct was so good at the museum.

DIRECTIONS: Write below the words you circled above. Use your dictionary to write the definitions.

	Word	Definition
1.	______________	______________________
2.	______________	______________________
3.	______________	______________________
4.	______________	______________________
5.	______________	______________________
6.	______________	______________________
7.	______________	______________________
8.	______________	______________________
9.	______________	______________________
10.	______________	______________________

Lesson 91 - Roots: spec & spect, mit & miss

Root	Word	Definition
spec, spect (see, look, examine)	inspector	someone who examines
mit, miss (send, let go)	dismissed	sent away

DIRECTIONS: In the sentences below, circle the root words with **spec**, **spect**, **mit**, and **miss**.

1. The Jesuit missionaries helped to civilize and settle much of the United States.
2. There are many financial speculators on Wall Street.
3. Are we permitted to stay up late because our pastor is visiting?
4. Many men became prospectors when gold was discovered in California.
5. Father did not want to dismiss the Bible students from the class.
6. The missile landed in the desert where it could do no harm.
7. The inspector visited the kitchen at the Trappist monastery to taste the fruitcake.
8. The spectators cheered when Babe Ruth hit a home run!

DIRECTIONS: Write the words in the above sentences with roots **spec**, **spect**, **mit**, or **miss**. Use your dictionary to write the definitions next to the words.

	Word	Definition
1.	____________	____________________
2.	____________	____________________
3.	____________	____________________
4.	____________	____________________
5.	____________	____________________
6.	____________	____________________
7.	____________	____________________
8.	____________	____________________

Lesson 92 - Roots: fac, fect, fic, & feit

The roots: **fac**, **fect**, **fic**, **feit** mean **do**, **make**, or **cause** as in **fac**tory.

DIRECTIONS: Read the words below. Notice the roots **fac**, **fect**, **fic**, or **feit** in each word.

defective	effect	factory	difficult
benefactor	fiction	facsimile	confection
counterfeit	perfect	fictitious	facility

DIRECTIONS: From the list above, write the correct word beside its definition.

1. ______________ having a problem or weakness
2. ______________ piece of writing about something made-up
3. ______________ something fake intended to fool people
4. ______________ hard to do
5. ______________ places where things can be made
6. ______________ person who does something kind or good
7. ______________ an imitation or exact copy
8. ______________ result; something caused by something else
9. ______________ without a mistake

DIRECTIONS: Write sentences using words from the list above.

1. ____
2. ____
3. ____
4. ____
5. ____
6. ____

Lesson 93 - Roots Review

DIRECTIONS: Find words from the roots you learned in Lessons 87-92 in the word search puzzle on this page. Circle the words, then write them on the lines below.

```
B A U D I E N C E J M A
L I J I N T R O D U C E
T A K Z S R C D E K Y B
S U B S C R I B E L T D
C D L P R E J E C T R I
M I S S I O N A R I E S
D O M O P R E D I C T M
E P O R T E R R H M C I
F H N M I S S A L N D S
G E X P O R T G I Z E S
S T W V N A B Z X P F H
```

1. ______ 2. ______ 3. ______

4. ______ 5. ______ 6. ______

7. ______ 8. ______ 9. ______

10. ______ 11. ______ 12. ______

DIRECTIONS: Write meaningful sentences using each word listed above.

1. ______
2. ______
3. ______
4. ______
5. ______
6. ______
7. ______
8. ______
9. ______
10. ______
11. ______
12. ______

Lesson 94 - Roots Review

DIRECTIONS: Read aloud the words listed below. Use the correct word to fill in the blanks.

portable	inspections	audio	dictators	ejected	missionaries
reduce	educators	permit	exported	predict	inscriptions

Over the last two hundred years, many Franciscan ________________________ came to the American continent. They came as ________________________ to teach the Indian people about God. They also taught them reading, arithmetic, and farming.

Jesuit priests also came. Some were killed in Mexico by cruel ___________________ who ruled for a short time. These rulers would not ________________________ the missionaries to help the poor because, as rulers, they were oppressors.

It would be easy to ______________________________ the fact that cruel rulers try to _____________________________ the influence of saintly priests and brothers. Priests in those days had ________________________ belongings as they were forced from their homes frequently. Everything they owned was packed on their horse or mule to travel from place to place. They travelled all over the southwest in both the American colonies and Mexico. European religious orders had ________________________ many of their finest priests to America.

________________________ of many of the old churches along the American-Mexican border show _______________________ on the tombs of these brave priests. At some of the old missions, one can listen to _______________________ tapes that tell the story of the priests. The tapes tell of how the priests were _______________________ from very successful missions by Protestant officials. After the priests were forced to leave, the missions fell apart. Governments would not provide the dedicated leadership needed to make these town-like areas run well. However, the skills that the priests taught the Indians remained.

Lesson 95 - Roots Review

DIRECTIONS: Read aloud the paragraphs below. Underline the words you have learned from the previous lessons, with the roots: **miss**, **duct**, **duc**, **dic**, **mit**, **port**, **script**, and **scribe**.

Father Junipero Serra

Father Junipero Serra was a Franciscan missionary who came to work in Mexico late in his life. No one would have ever predicted that this successful college professor would become "God's Little Walker" in the wilds of California. Fr. Serra's first job in Mexico was as an educator. He taught in the college. He knew he must do more. He begged to be permitted to go north and help the California Indians. He dismissed the idea that he was too old and sick to go.

Fr. Serra took chickens, goats, cows, and mules, as well as bags of grain, on his trip north. He walked from Mexico City to what is today Carmel, California. He set up missions and introduced farming to the warlike Indians. He taught them to conduct their lives according to the Will of God. The Indians built houses around the missions. The farms flourished. Killing among the Indians was reduced and replaced with a calm, peaceful comportment taught them by Fr. Serra.

With his portable belongings packed on a little mule, Fr. Serra walked thousands of miles from mission to mission preaching, teaching, baptizing, and offering Mass for his beloved Indians. Fr. Serra loved his Indian converts so much that once, when a vindictive viceroy acting as a dictator hurt the Indians, Fr. Serra walked from Carmel to Mexico City to complain. Because of his description of the injustice, the viceroy was dismissed. A new viceroy was appointed to serve at Fr. Serra's discretion. Fr. Serra died at his Carmel mission. His grave is inscribed with a prayer for his beloved Indians.

DIRECTIONS: Write below the words you underlined in the story above. If a word is repeated, write it only once.

____________	____________	____________
____________	____________	____________
____________	____________	____________
____________	____________	____________
____________	____________	____________
____________		

Lesson 96 - Compound Words

Rule: Two or more complete words together form a new word. It is called a **compound word**.

Examples: **blackboard, shipmate**

DIRECTIONS: Write the two words in the compound words below.

1. housetop = **house** + **top**
2. churchyard = ________ + ________
3. doorkeeper = ________ + ________
4. football = ________ + ________
5. godfather = ________ + ________
6. grandmother = ________ + ________
7. racecourse = ________ + ________
8. horseback = ________ + ________

DIRECTIONS: Write 20 other compound words you can find in a dictionary.

1. ________
2. ________
3. ________
4. ________
5. ________
6. ________
7. ________
8. ________
9. ________
10. ________
11. ________
12. ________
13. ________
14. ________
15. ________
16. ________
17. ________
18. ________
19. ________
20. ________

Lesson 97 - Compound Words

DIRECTIONS: Read aloud the list words. Then write the proper compound word to fill in the blanks.

waterpots	grandfather	priesthood	bluebird	godmother
firemen	Eastertime	storehouse	highways	choirmaster

1. At Cana, Jesus changed the water in the ____________________ into wine.
2. The ____________________ gave inspiration for the song *Over the Rainbow*.
3. The ____________________taught his grandchildren how to say their prayers.
4. The lilies on the altar were very beautiful and fragrant at ______________________.
5. The _________________ held my baby brother during the Baptism ceremony.
6. The ___________________________ taught the children to sing Gregorian Chant.
7. The ___________________ volunteered to help the priest repair the burned church.
8. The five candidates for the ______________________ will be ordained next Sunday.
9. The ravens neither sow nor reap nor have a ___________________, but God feeds them.
10. The Lord said, "Go out into the ______________________ and tell them to come in, that My house may be filled."

DIRECTIONS: Make compound words by drawing a line from words in the first column to words in the second column.

1. life	man	11. land	break
2. ear	set	12. grand	coat
3. police	ball	13. mountain	cake
4. earth	vine	14. cup	milk
5. sun	muff	15. fish	mother
6. grape	worm	16. butter	hook
7. moth	bread	17. moon	slide
8. ginger	time	18. rain	quake
9. down	groom	19. earth	top
10. bride	pour	20. heart	light

Lesson 98 - Compound Words

DIRECTIONS: Match the word in Column A with the correct word in Column B that will make a compound word. Write the word in the space at the end of the columns.

	Column A	Column B	
1.	brief	meal	____________
2.	earth	groom	____________
3.	grape	case	____________
4.	class	fruit	____________
5.	bride	mate	____________
6.	oat	track	____________
7.	race	worm	____________
8.	see	saw	____________

DIRECTIONS: Draw a vertical line to separate the words in the compound words below.

1. sunlight
2. bookmark
3. nutcracker
4. outdoor
5. bedspread
6. outline
7. newspaper
8. overnight
9. paperhanger
10. parkway
11. rattlesnake
12. redhead
13. ringmaster
14. roadblock
15. roommate
16. stockyard

DIRECTIONS: Write a sentence for any four of the words above.

1. ____

2. ____

3. ____

4. ____

Lesson 99 - Possessives

Rule: To show possession or ownership, add an **apostrophe** and **s**.

Examples:
The priest has a green stole.
The priest**'s** stole is green. (**Possessive**)
The **'s** after "priest" shows he owns the stole.

Rule: If a word ends in **s**, the apostrophe comes after the **s**.

Examples:
The statue belongs to the Jones family.
The Jones' painting was blessed by Father Edwards. (**Possessive**)

DIRECTIONS: Change the sentences below to show possession.

---

1. The rosary belonging to Father was blessed by Pope Benedict XVI.

   ____

2. The garments of Jesus became white as snow.

   ____

3. The face of Jesus shone as bright as the sun.

   ____

4. The Franciscan Brothers have robes that are made of brown wool.

   ____

5. The green scapular, which belongs to James, is on the dresser.

   ____

6. The work of Victoria kept her busy over the weekend.

   ____

7. Jesus entered the house of Peter and cured the mother of his wife.

   ____

8. Those fields, which adjoin the monastery, are owned by the Benedictines.

   ____

9. Jonah was in the belly of the whale three days and three nights.

   ____

10. The brass band of Canada played a traditional religious hymn.

    ____

Lesson 100 - Possessives

Rule: To make a noun show possession, add **'s** to a singular noun.

To a plural noun not ending in **s**, add **'s**.
To a plural noun ending in **s**, add only an apostrophe (**'**).

Sally**'s** hat: possessive for a singular noun
people**'s** government: possessive for a plural noun not ending in s
soldiers**'** coats: possessive for a plural noun ending in s

DIRECTIONS: Make possessives of the following words.

women	______________	boys	______________
bats	______________	cats	______________
mother	______________	Tom	______________
children	______________	men	______________
parents	______________	father	______________

DIRECTIONS**:** Write one sentence using a possessive plural ending in **s**, and a sentence using a possessive plural not ending in **s**.

1. ____

____

2. ____

____

DIRECTIONS: Change the underlined plural words in the sentences below to plural possessives. Write the new words in the spaces provided.

1. The <u>popes</u> encyclicals reaffirm the Immaculate Conception. ______________
2. The <u>churches</u> altars were profusely decorated with flowers. ______________
3. The <u>saints</u> relics were protected in glass cases. ______________
4. The <u>sheep</u> bleats went unheeded by the shepherds. ______________
5. The <u>crews</u> oars became mixed up during the race. ______________

Lesson 101 - Contractions

Rule: A **contraction** is a short way of writing two words as one. It is made by putting two words together and leaving out some of the letters. An apostrophe is used in place of the missing letters.

Words	Contraction	Words	Contraction	Words	Contraction
can not ___	can't	I am ___	I'm	you are ___	you're
will not ___	won't	he will ___	he'll	let us ___	let's

DIRECTIONS: Read the contraction. Write the full two words on the line next to it.

I'll ______________________ I'm ______________________

you'll ______________________ you're ______________________

she'll ______________________ I've ______________________

he'll ______________________ you've ______________________

it'll ______________________ they've ______________________

DIRECTIONS: Write out the contractions of these groups of two words.

we are ______________________ they will ______________________

that is ______________________ let us ______________________

is not ______________________ could not ______________________

can not ______________________ would not ______________________

DIRECTIONS: Write ten sentences containing contractions.

1. ____
2. ____
3. ____
4. ____
5. ____
6. ____
7. ____
8. ____
9. ____
10. ____

Lesson 102 - Contractions

Rule: A contraction is a short way to write two words as one. The **apostrophe** replaces one or more letters to make two words one.

DIRECTIONS: Read the following contractions. Write the two words which the contraction represents.

	Contraction	two words	Contraction	two words
1.	can't	____________	didn't	____________
2.	she'll	____________	we'll	____________
3.	isn't	____________	it's	____________
4.	that's	____________	I've	____________
5.	we've	____________	you've	____________
6.	we're	____________	let's	____________
7.	you're	____________	he's	____________
8.	they're	____________	don't	____________
9.	they'll	____________	doesn't	____________
10.	wouldn't	____________	didn't	____________
11.	I'm	____________	hadn't	____________
12.	he'll	____________	wasn't	____________

DIRECTIONS: Write a sentence for six of the contractions above.

1. ____________________________
2. ____________________________
3. ____________________________
4. ____________________________
5. ____________________________
6. ____________________________

Lesson 103 - Contractions

DIRECTIONS: Underline all the contractions in the following story.

Margaret Clitherow

Young Margaret wasn't thinking of marriage when she went to the butcher shop for her mother. Mr. Clitherow, the butcher, was a nice young man, but she hadn't been giving him a second look. The butcher, however, liked the sweet, happy, little Margaret. He didn't speak much to her at first. As time went by, though, the shy butcher and the sweet girl became friends.

Mr. Clitherow didn't speak to Margaret about marriage. He spoke to her father first. In Elizabethan England, the marriage was always arranged for the girl. Margaret couldn't have been happier about her father's choice of a husband. Mr. Clitherow was a good man, and he would prove how good after the marriage.

Both the Clitherows were Anglican. There weren't many Catholics in England then, as it was against the law. However, the young bride met several Catholics in York where they lived. She was so impressed that she converted. Her husband didn't object. Then she began to do more. She wouldn't let the children go unschooled, so she taught catechism in her home. She hid priests in her attic. She'd get arrested time after time for protecting Catholics. Her husband always sent bail to free her. That's the kind of man he was.

Finally, Margaret was sentenced to death. "I'll see you in Heaven," she told her husband. He wept uncontrollably as he saw the large, heavy door placed on top of her frail body. As each layer of rock crushed the life out of her, she prayed, "God help England and my family."

DIRECTIONS: Write the words in the story that you underlined.

1. ____________________
2. ____________________
3. ____________________
4. ____________________
5. ____________________
6. ____________________
7. ____________________
8. ____________________
9. ____________________
10. ____________________
11. ____________________

Lesson 104 - Contractions, Possessives, and Compound Words

DIRECTIONS: Read the story aloud. Note the words that need apostrophes and place the apostrophes in the proper place. Underline the compound words.

Mother Seton

Elizabeth Bailey was born in New York City. As a child, shed often watch the sunset and daydream by the small waterfall near her house. This little Protestant girl couldnt have imagined that someday she would be a Roman Catholic saint.

Her familys attendance at the local Episcopal church was a Sunday ritual. Here Elizabeth met her future husband. Mr. Seton was a very rich, successful businessman. The Setons family life was the same as all wealthy New Yorkers. Social life and volunteer work filled Elizabeths time. As her children were born, she became more of a homebody. Until her husband became ill, Elizabeth didnt enjoy anything more than spending evenings at home with her husband and their five children.

Mr. Setons illness changed that. "Hell be better off with a change of scenery," the doctor said. So they travelled with one daughter to Italy to stay with Catholic friends. Sadly, soon after they arrived in Italy, Mr. Seton died. Elizabeth and her daughter remained there. Her Catholic friends faithful devotion impressed her. Elizabeth decided to become a Catholic. When she returned home to America, she was baptized. Her family disowned her because of this. Without their financial help, her situation was desperate.

To support her children, Elizabeth began a school. Soon Elizabeth was teaching in Emmitsburg, Maryland. There she founded the order of the Sisters of Charity. Doubtless, the work of these sisters in Catholic schools and hospitals helped to spread the Faith in America. Some time after her death, Mother Seton was canonized.

DIRECTIONS: Write the compound words, possessives, and contractions you found in the story.

compound words	possessives	contractions
__________	__________	__________
__________	__________	__________
__________	__________	__________
__________	__________	__________
__________	__________	
__________		
__________		
__________		

Lesson 105 - Contractions, Possessives, and Compound Words

DIRECTIONS: On the line at the right, tell whether each phrase contains a **contraction, possessive,** or a **compound word**.

1. Jesus' apostles ______________________
2. let's pray ______________________
3. Church doorway ______________________
4. Yuletide cheer ______________________
5. just a figurehead ______________________
6. Christ's cross ______________________
7. wouldn't sin ______________________
8. Mary's heart ______________________

DIRECTIONS: Write sentences on the lines below using 5 contractions and 5 possessives.

1. ____
2. ____
3. ____
4. ____
5. ____
6. ____
7. ____
8. ____
9. ____
10. ____

Lesson 106 - Suffixes for Comparison: er & est

Definition: A suffix is a word part added to the end of a word or root, the basic word part.

Rule: Adjectives usually show comparison by adding the suffix **er** or **est** to the word or root. When comparing two things, add **er**, the comparative form. When comparing more than two things, add **est**, the superlative form.

Rule: When adding suffixes, sometimes there needs to be a change in the ending of the word or root.

1. When a short-vowel word ends in a single consonant, usually double the consonant before adding the suffix **er** or **est**. **Example**: hot, hotter, hottest
2. When a word ends in silent e, drop the e before adding **er** or **est**. **Example**: wise, wiser, wisest
3. When a word ends in **y** preceded by a consonant, change the **y** to **i** before adding **er** or **est**. **Example**: holy, holier, holiest

---

DIRECTIONS: Circle the correct word.

---

1. It was the (pretty, prettier, prettiest) church I ever saw.
2. The red tulips seem (large, larger, largest) than the yellow tulips.
3. The organ sounds (loud, louder, loudest) than the one at Saint Patrick's.
4. She has the (neat, neater, neatest) house in town!
5. The weatherman said it was the (cold, colder, coldest) day of the year.
6. It was (hot, hotter, hottest) today than yesterday.
7. Jim said that mountain was the (high, higher, highest) of the two.
8. Sally thought Mary was the (friendly, friendlier, friendliest) girl in her dance class.
9. He is not (heavy, heavier, heaviest), Father, he is my brother.
10. St. John the Beloved was the (young, younger, youngest) of the Apostles.
11. The homeschoolers gave food to the (poor, poorer, poorest) families in town.
12. The monks thought St. Joseph of Cupertino was the (humble, humbler, humblest) man in the monastery.

Lesson 107 - Suffixes: er & est

DIRECTIONS: Select four of the **simple** forms of the adjectives from Lesson 106. Write a sentence using each of the four words.

1. ______________________________
2. ______________________________
3. ______________________________
4. ______________________________

DIRECTIONS: Write four sentences using the **comparative** forms of four adjectives.

1. ______________________________
2. ______________________________
3. ______________________________
4. ______________________________

DIRECTIONS: Write four sentences using the **superlative** forms of four adjectives.

1. ______________________________
2. ______________________________
3. ______________________________
4. ______________________________

Lesson 108 - Suffixes: er & est

Rule: Adjectives usually show comparison by adding the suffixes **er** or **est** to the root.

When comparing two things, add **er**, the comparative form.
When comparing more than two things, add **est**, the superlative form.

Example:

Simple	Comparative	Superlative
weak	weaker	weakest

DIRECTIONS: Circle the word to complete the sentences below.

1. That is the (kind, kinder, kindest) priest I ever met.
2. Queen Juliana was (tall, taller, tallest) than Queen Elizabeth.
3. Her dessert tasted (sweet, sweeter, sweetest) than the chef's.
4. Samson proved he was (strong, stronger, strongest) than the evil Philistines.

DIRECTIONS: Write the adjectives in the comparative and superlative forms.

	Simple	Comparative	Superlative
1.	dirty	__________	__________
2.	large	__________	__________
3.	late	__________	__________
4.	early	__________	__________

DIRECTIONS: Write three sentences using one **simple,** one **comparative,** and one **superlative** adjective formed by adding the suffix **er** or **est**.

1. Simple

____

2. Comparative

____

3. Superlative

____

Lesson 109 - Suffixes: er, or, & ist

Rule: When suffixes are added to the end of a root word, the meaning of the word will change.

Suffixes **er** and **or** mean **someone or something that can do something**. It can change a verb to a noun.

The suffix **ist** can mean **someone who does something**. This suffix changes one noun into another kind of noun.

Suffix	**Verb**	**Noun**	**Suffix**	**Noun**	**Noun**
er	play	player	ist	violin	violinist
	teach	teacher		piano	pianist
or	act	actor			
	imitate	imitator			

DIRECTIONS: Make a verb into a noun by adding the suffix **er** or **or**. If the word ends in **e**, drop the **e** before adding the suffix. Write the noun on the line above the verb.

1. Damian wanted to be a ______________________ in the vineyard of Our Lord.
   work
2. G.K. Chesterton, author of the book *Orthodoxy*, was a Catholic ______________________.
   write
3. St. Dominic was a great ______________________ and ______________________ of the Dominican Order.
   preach, found
4. Michelangelo, who was a ______________________, also painted the beautiful Sistine Chapel ceiling.
   sculpt
5. Were you ever a ______________________ at the Vatican?
   visit

DIRECTIONS: To each root word, add **ist** to change the word. If the word ends in a **vowel** or **y**, drop it before adding **ist**.

1. Someone who settled in this country when there were still thirteen colonies, is known as a ______________________.
   colony
2. A great ______________________ is able to weave more truth than fiction into his story.
   novel
3. The ______________________ in our church loves to play old Latin hymns.
   organ
4. The Jewish author, Franz Werfel, planned to be only a ______________________ at Lourdes but eventually became a Catholic.
   tour
5. Each year, my brother fixes up his bicycle and joins the annual ______________________ race.
   bicycle

Lesson 110 - Suffixes: ee, ent, ant, & eer

Rule: Suffixes **ee, ent,** and **ant** mean **someone who** or **that which**. The suffix **eer** usually means **someone who**.

Suffix	Root Word	New Word	Suffix	Root Word	New Word
ee	appoint	appointee	eer	engine	engineer
ent	depend	dependent	ant	protest	Protestant

DIRECTIONS: Define the words below. Use your dictionary if necessary.

1. appointee:

   ____

2. dependent:

   ____

3. Protestant:

   ____

4. engineer:

   ____

DIRECTIONS: Add the proper suffix which will make the word properly complete the sentence. Check the dictionary for the correct spelling.

1. If you don't know the facts, you are ____________________ of them.
   ignore
2. Raphael is an ____________________ of that store.
   employ
3. Be careful! That spray is an insect ____________________.
   repel
4. People who climb mountains are called ____________________.
   mountain
5. Joan likes to have it known that she is a ____________________ of George Washington.
   descend
6. St. Timothy was an ____________________ of St. Paul.
   assist
7. The president's ____________________ was not confirmed by the Senate.
   appoint
8. Because he was out of town, he voted by ____________________ ballot.
   absent
9. The Trappist monks prayed for the ____________________ who tried to take their land.
   claim
10. The Cure of Ars became a popular spiritual ____________________ and confessor.
    consult

Lesson 111 - Suffixes: ward, en, & ize

DIRECTIONS: A suffix added to a root word makes a new word. Add **ward, en,** or **ize** to the root word that completes the sentences below.

1. The Visitation Sisters were nearing the end of their vacation time as they headed ________________________.
   home
2. Large ________________________ scapulars were worn often by monks.
   wool
3. Would you ________________________ the name cards for me, please?
   alphabet
4. The army moved ________________________ to meet the enemy.
   fore
5. If you drag an issue into the political discussion, you ________________________ the issue.
   politic
6. Mother Theresa added more cloth to the bottom of the habit to ________________________ it for the novice.
   length
7. We are going to install a new kitchen to help ________________________ the convent for the Franciscan Sisters.
   modern
8. Dad had to ________________________ the screw to secure the shelf.
   tight
9. Little Blessed Imelda watched with awe and love as the priest raised the ________________________ chalice at the moment of Consecration.
   gold
10. If you want to see the meteor shower, you will have to look ________________________.
    east

DIRECTIONS: Write the words you made under the proper suffix heading.

ward	**en**	**ize**
________	________	________
________	________	________
________	________	________
	________	

Lesson 112 - Suffixes: ful & ness

Rule: The suffix **ful** added to a root usually makes the word a noun or an adjective. The suffix **ness** added to a root usually makes the word a noun.

Suffix	Root	Word	Part of speech
ful	help	helpful	adjective
ful	hand	handful	noun
ness	loud	loudness	noun

DIRECTIONS: Read the list words aloud. Use a dictionary to look up any word you do not understand. Write the correct words to complete the sentences.

cleanliness	pocketful	weakness	faithful
successful	bucketful	Godliness	armful
friendliness	spoonful	wonderful	harmful

1. The old proverb is, "____________________ is next to ____________________."
2. As she began to sort the laundry, Mother discovered a ____________________ of pennies in Johnny's trousers.
3. Because it contains lead, paint can be very ____________________ to children who swallow it.
4. "Just a ____________________ of sugar helps the medicine go down in the most delightful way!"
5. The ____________________ businessman liked to fly first class.
6. The devil plays on our ____________________ to tempt us to sin.
7. The children picked a ____________________ of blueberries while they were on the picnic.
8. Good Catholics are ____________________ to the Church's teachings.
9. The ____________________ of the Indians made for a ____________________ trip down the river.
10. Each nun carried an ____________________ of the St. Gregory Hymnals to give to the choir members.

Lesson 113 - Suffixes: ful & ness

DIRECTIONS: Complete the sentences by writing the best word.

1. The ________________________ worship Our Lord at Mass every Sunday.

   faith faithful faithless

2. A truly __________________ man is known by his humility.

   great greater greatness

3. Because she would not give up Christianity, St. Apollonia lost a __________________ of teeth during her persecution.

   mouth mouths mouthful

4. St. John Vianney, the Curé of Ars, was known for his ________________.

   holy holiness holiest

5. The rose bouquet on the May altar was _________________ than the daisy one.

   lovely lovelier loveliest

6. St. Vincent de Paul, who was known for ministering to the poor, was ________________ to all who called on him.

   help helpful helped

7. A mark of a Christian gentleman is ______________________.

   polite politely politeness

8. Because Christine is such a ________________ person, everyone loves her.

   kind kindly kindness

9. Graces are ___________________ for those who receive the sacraments.

   plenty plentiful plural

10. We should all be ___________________ for the gift of Faith that we received at Baptism.

    thank thankful thanks

11. We were filled with ____________________ as we studied the history of the Cathedral of Notre Dame.

    happy happiness happier

12. The Danube River is one of the most ___________________ places in Austria.

    beauty beautiful beautious

Lesson 114 - Suffixes Review

DIRECTIONS: You have studied suffixes in this unit. Read the story below and underline the words that contain the suffixes you have learned in this unit: **ant, ee, eer, en, ent, er, est, ful, ist, ize, ness, or,** and **ward**.

The New Yorker

Little Mary Quinn was born in New York City. She was a sweet, helpful child who looked forward to going to daily Mass at St. Patrick's Cathedral. As she walked the seven blocks from her First Avenue tenement apartment to church, she often would meet a visitor in distress. Mary would give directions for walking, or going by bus or subway. The person would smile at this little assistant. They would thank her for her kindness and leave, confident of the way.

As Mary walked westward, she looked skyward at the cathedral spires. As the sun rose, the shadows of the spires would shorten. She could tell by the shadows how long it would be before Mass. She wasn't dependent on a watch for she didn't own one. As she passed the Fifth Avenue shops, an employee here and there would wave "hello." Of all the shopkeepers, the barber was the funniest. He always had a joke or a trick to make Mary laugh.

The subway engineer on his way to Mass would say, "Hurry up, Mary, the organist will start the music before you get there!" He knew Mary liked to be on time for the processional hymn. Mary loved to see all the different people come into St. Patrick's. The old actor, the basketball player, and the businessmen and women all came with faithful reverence to start their day with the Holy Sacrifice of the Mass.

Mary thought New York must be the best example of a civilized Catholic society. Unfortunately, Mary lived many years ago. If she would awaken to go to Mass today, she would not find New York or the rest of the world so full of happiness.

DIRECTIONS: Write some of the words you underlined in the story.

1. ______	8. ______	15. ______
2. ______	9. ______	16. ______
3. ______	10. ______	17. ______
4. ______	11. ______	18. ______
5. ______	12. ______	19. ______
6. ______	13. ______	20. ______
7. ______	14. ______	21. ______
		22. ______

Lesson 115 - Suffixes: hood, ship, & ment

Rule: The suffixes **hood, ship** and **ment** usually mean the **state of being**. Added to a noun, they change the meaning of the root word.

Suffix	**Root**	**New word**
hood	brother	brotherhood
ship	friend	friendship
ment	excite	excitement

DIRECTIONS: Read the list words aloud. Write a definition for the root word on line **a** and a definition for the new word (root + suffix) on line **b**. Use a dictionary.

partnership	falsehood	agreement	priesthood	championship
equipment	township	sisterhood	impediment	

1. a. ______________________________

   b. ______________________________

2. a. ______________________________

   b. ______________________________

3. a. ______________________________

   b. ______________________________

4. a. ______________________________

   b. ______________________________

5. a. ______________________________

   b. ______________________________

6. a. ______________________________

   b. ______________________________

7. a. ______________________________

   b. ______________________________

8. a. ______________________________

   b. ______________________________

9. a. ______________________________

   b. ______________________________

Lesson 116 - Suffixes: hood, ship, & ment

DIRECTIONS: Use the suffixes **hood, ship,** or **ment** to make new words using the list below. Write the word with the correct suffix to complete each sentence.

relation	priest	governor	place	retire	child	steward
partner	move	neighbor	owner	false	judge	command

1. He showed the deed that proved ______________________ of the house.
2. Jane Eyre spent her ______________________ in an orphanage.
3. The paralyzed man at the pool of Bethsaida yelled with joy when there was ______________________ in his legs.
4. People who tell ______________________ are usually trapped by their own lies.
5. Children should have a good ______________________ with their parents.
6. The governor resigned the ______________________ because of ill health.
7. Did you take a ______________________ test when you entered high school?
8. Boys who think they are called to serve God in the ______________________, should pray for God's will.
9. St. Jerome led a life of ______________________ from the world in order to be closer to God.
10. The business ______________________ between the two brothers was very successful.
11. Jesus told a story about an unjust steward who was removed from his ______________________.
12. Catholic families can evangelize right in their own ______________________ by being good examples.
13. Jesus said that the most important ______________________ is to love God above all else and love your neighbor as yourself.
14. At the end of the world, each soul will be judged by Christ; therefore, that time is called the Final ______________________.

Lesson 117 - Suffixes: able & ible

Rule: Suffixes **able** and **ible** mean **able to be** or **full of**.

Suffix	**Root**	**New Word**
able	adore	adorable
ible	convert	convertible

DIRECTIONS: Read the list words below aloud. Use your dictionary to look up the meanings of any words you don't know. Complete the sentences with the correct word.

horrible	reversible	eatable	profitable	incorruptible
reliable	defensible	sensible	breakable	curable

1. The mothers liked Sally to baby-sit because she was so ________________________.
2. Francisco and Jacinta could not begin to describe their vision of hell; it was too ________________________.
3. It is not ________________________ to cross the street between parked cars.
4. Mother purchased the coat because it was________________________.
5. The fortress was ________________________ because it was built on the edge of a cliff and was heavily armed.
6. The pizza was so spicy, it was not________________________.
7. St. Catherine Laboure's body can still be seen today because it is __________________.
8. The salesman promised the plastic toy was not ________________________.
9. Sadly, many people think that problems are ________________________ with money.
10. Jesus taught it is not ________________________ for a man to gain the whole world but suffer the eternal loss of his soul.

Lesson 118 - Suffixes: able & ible

DIRECTIONS: Underline the words in the sentences below that contain the suffixes **able** and **ible**.

1. The stigmatist priest, Saint Padre Pio, helped a little girl with an incurable disease.
2. St. Kateri Tekakwitha was charitable to all, even to her Indian persecutors.
3. The old Franciscan habits were still usable to be cut up for scapulars.
4. I felt horrible after eating too much pizza.
5. The Boston Symphony presented an enjoyable Christmas concert.
6. The lovable toddler hugged her father when he came home.
7. Nothing is impossible with God.
8. The armored tank seemed indestructible against the enemy fire.
9. Most Sweet and Adorable Jesus, please listen to my prayer.

DIRECTIONS: Write definitions for the words below. Use your dictionary.

	Word	*Definition*
1.	breakable	______________________________
2.	memorable	______________________________
3.	knowable	______________________________
4.	laughable	______________________________
5.	remarkable	______________________________
6.	incredible	______________________________
7.	sensible	______________________________
8.	responsible	______________________________
9.	inflexible	______________________________

Lesson 119 - Suffixes: ion, ation, ition, & tion

Rule: Suffixes **ion**, **ation**, **ition**, and **tion** mean **the condition of being**.

Suffix	**Root**	**New Word**
ion	adopt	adoption
ation	dictate	dictation
ition	compose	composition
tion	afflict	affliction

DIRECTIONS: Read the word list. Write the correct word to complete the sentences. Use your dictionary if you are unsure of any of the meanings.

Visitation	invitation	confirmation	intercession	addition	imagination
ordination	Contrition	Presentation	veneration	devotion	consecration

1. We say an Act of ______________________ at the end of Confession.
2. The Second Joyful Mystery of the Rosary is the ______________________.
3. We ask for the Blessed Mother's ______________________ when we want favors from Her Son, Jesus.
4. I learned ______________________ when I was in first grade.
5. We were sent an ______________________ to my aunt's wedding.
6. At His ______________________, Jesus was held in the arms of Simeon.
7. Almost everyone in Sacred Heart parish attended Father Snyder's ______________________.
8. The bishop came to St. Patrick's for the eighth graders'______________________.
9. Edgar Allen Poe's short stories are famous for their ______________________.
10. Most Catholics have a great ______________________ to the Blessed Virgin Mary.
11. All should kneel at the ______________________ of the Mass.
12. Saints are held in ______________________, not adoration.

Lesson 120 - Suffixes: ion, tion, ation, & ition

Rule: If a word ends in **e** or **y**, drop the **e** or **y** before adding the suffix **ion, tion, ation,** or **ition**.

DIRECTIONS: Read the sentences. Complete the sentences by writing the word that is most appropriate. Notice that the **e** or **y** is dropped before adding the suffix.

1. The second step to being declared a saint is ____________________.

   beatify beatification

2. The ____________________ of representatives to the United Nations meets in New York.

   delegate delegation

3. When you say the Rosary, you should ____________________ on the mystery.

   meditate meditation

4. We must attend Mass on all holy days of ____________________.

   obligate obligation

5. Charitable organizations must depend on ____________________ to continue their work.

   donate donations

6. What was the ____________________ for that act?

   justify justification

7. We sent ____________________ to our relatives for Sarah's First Holy Communion.

   invite invitations

DIRECTIONS: Drop the final **e**, then add suffixes **ion, tion, ation,** or **ition** to make new words.

1. confuse ____________________
2. radiate ____________________
3. civilize ____________________
4. realize ____________________
5. quote ____________________
6. compose ____________________
7. obligate ____________________
8. capitalize ____________________
9. celebrate ____________________
10. persecute ____________________

Lesson 121 - Suffixes: ance, ence, ive, & ity

Rule: Suffixes **ance, ence,** and **ity** usually mean **the state of being** or **quality**.

The suffix **ive** means **having to do with** or **likely to**.

Suffix	Root	New word
ance	resemble	resemblance
ence	confide	confidence
ity	sensitive	sensitivity
ive	act	active

DIRECTIONS: Read each question. Circle the word that best answers the question.

1. When we are sure of ourselves, we are said to have what?

   confidence massive

2. What is the small voice inside us which tells us when we are doing wrong?

   temperance conscience

3. Someone's natural disposition or characteristics is also called what?

   votive personality

4. What removes the temporal punishment due to sin?

   impressive indulgence

5. When we are honest in dealing with people, we are said to have what?

   sincerity temperance

6. When a writer is clever in writing new plots, we can say he is what?

   creative acceptance

7. What is a lack of knowledge called?

   charity ignorance

8. What do you call a person who cares about another's problems?

   sensitive votive

9. What do we call a commanding sentence?

   imperative active

10. Signs are posted on roads near low overhead bridges to warn trucks that there might not be enough what?

    clearance turbulence

Lesson 122 - Suffixes: ance, ence, ive, & ity

Rule: The suffixes **ance**, **ence**, and **ity** usually mean **the quality** or **state of being**.

The suffix **ive** usually means **likely to** or **having to do with**.

An **analogy** tells how one thing is related to another.
Example: **priest** is to **man** as **nun** is to **woman**
happy is to **joyful** as **unhappy** is to **sad**
sin is to **virtue** as **evil** is to **good**

DIRECTIONS: Circle the correct word to finish the **analogy**. Use your dictionary, if necessary.

1. **Generosity** is to **stinginess** as ______________________ is to **independence**.

   charity   reliance   sensitive

2. **Disturbance** is to **noise** as **peacefulness** is to ______________________.

   publicity   quiet   originality

3. **Charity** is to **kindness** as ______________________ is to **lying**.

   explosive   deceit   acceptance

4. **Patience** is to **long-suffering** as ______________________ is to **quick-tempered.**

   volatile   sincerity   decorative

5. ______________________ is to **sin** as **medicine** is to **illness**.

   penance   positive   dependence

6. **Person** is to **humanity** as **king** is to ______________________.

   nobility   importance   attendance

7. ______________________ is to **counterfeit** as **energetic** is to **lethargic**.

   purity   authenticity   difference

8. **Generator** is to ______________________ as **artist** is to **sculpture**.

   punitive   electricity   indulgence

9. **Temperance** is to **drunkenness** as ______________________ is to **ignorance**.

   chastity   charity   knowledge

10. **Lavishness** is to **plenty** as ______________________ is to **poverty**.

    confidence   austerity   originality

Lesson 123 - Suffixes Review

DIRECTIONS: Read the story. Find words that use the suffixes **able, ance, ation, ence, hood, ible, ion, ition, ity, ive, ment,** and **ship**. Circle the words.

Sisterhood

Some women have the courage to make the commitment to be Brides of Christ by entering a convent. They find a special kind of spiritual friendship with God. Their sacrifice and penance help grace to flow into a very insensitive, disabled world. They give up their independence, and replace it with fidelity and obedience. This calls attention to the possibility of living a life of dedication. Women are still capable of making such sacrifices.

If you know women who have joined the sisterhood of religious life and are faithful and obedient, you are truly fortunate. Never fail to give them the recognition and respect they deserve. Join in the celebration of their vocations. Say "Thank you, Sister," for their generosity. Pray for them. Ask God for many more such courageous women. Remember, girls, whatever your vocation in life, women are the foundation of civilization. Always emulate Mary. Good women make a good society.

DIRECTIONS: Below, write the words you have circled.

1.	________	11.	________
2.	________	12.	________
3.	________	13.	________
4.	________	14.	________
5.	________	15.	________
6.	________	16.	________
7.	________	17.	________
8.	________	18.	________
9.	________	19.	________
10.	________	20.	________

Lesson 124 - Suffix Review

DIRECTIONS: Read aloud the following words.

player	bucketful	horrible
teacher	faithless	reliable
actor	greater	reversible
irritator	mouthful	defensible
violinist	holiness	breakable
pianist	loveliest	profitable
appointee	helpful	sensible
dependent	politeness	curable
engineer	plentiful	enjoyable
woolen	beautiful	adoption
homework	wonderful	dictation
modernize	friendship	composition
tighten	excitement	affliction
cleanliness	partnership	imagination
pocketful	championship	contrition
Godliness	township	ordination
successful	equipment	devotion
friendliness	falsehood	veneration

Lesson 125 - Suffixes: Doubling the Final Consonant

Rule: When a short-vowel word or syllable ends in a single consonant, usually double the consonant before adding a suffix that begins with a vowel.

Example: dip, dipped

DIRECTIONS: Form new words below by putting each root and suffix together. Write the new words on the lines.

1. wash + ing ____________
2. refer + ing ____________
3. pray + ing ____________
4. sad + est ____________
5. din + er ____________
6. part + ed ____________
7. sleep + ing ____________
8. hard + er ____________
9. swim + ing ____________
10. knit + ing ____________
11. worship + ed ____________
12. walk + er ____________
13. kind + est ____________
14. beg + ing ____________
15. grab + ed ____________
16. learn + ing ____________
17. pat + ed ____________
18. sin + er ____________
19. stop + ed ____________
20. get + ing ____________

DIRECTIONS: Read aloud the sentences. Draw a circle around each word that doubles the final consonant to add a suffix. Then write its root on the line.

1. John is planning to go to confession this Saturday. ____________
2. Some bystanders were stunned at the Roman soldiers' cruelty toward Jesus. ____________
3. Sarah is wrapping a Christmas present for her mother. ____________
4. The members of the Sanhedrin plotted against Jesus. ____________
5. Easter Sunday was one of the hottest days of the year. ____________
6. Two robbers were crucified the same day as Jesus. ____________

Lesson 126 - Suffixes: Doubling the Final Consonant

Rule: When a word with a short vowel ends in a single consonant, usually double the consonant before adding a suffix that begins with a vowel.

DIRECTIONS: Form new words by putting each root and suffix together. Write the new words on the lines.

can + ing	____________	rip + ing	____________
fat + est	____________	mad + ness	____________
let + er	____________	plant + ed	____________
equip + ment	____________	sharp + ness	____________
pad + ed	____________	snip + ing	____________
relent + less	____________	prayer + ful	____________
man + ed	____________	sweet + est	____________
quick + ly	____________	stop + ed	____________

DIRECTIONS: Read the words and sentences below aloud. Circle the root in each word in the list. Then complete each sentence with a word from the list.

grabbing	dripped	snapping	sinners	rubbing
winner	wrapping	canning	ripped	stopped

1. The children of Fatima offered sacrifices for the conversion of ____________.
2. Blood ____________ from Christ's hands and feet as He hung on the Cross.
3. The high priest ____________ his garment in protest against the words of Jesus.
4. Watch out for that ____________ turtle!
5. Mary was the ____________ in the creative writing contest.
6. ____________ the suntan lotion on her arms protected her from being burned.
7. We were ____________ her presents yesterday.
8. They ____________ shopping at the expensive store.
9. Mother spends a whole week ____________ the fruits and vegetables.
10. Don't be ____________ all the cookies, children!

Lesson 127 - Suffixes: Dropping the Final e

Rule: When a word ends in final **e**, drop the **e** before adding a suffix that begins with a vowel.

Example: tape, taping

DIRECTIONS: Form new words by adding the suffixes **es**, **ed**, and **ing** to the words below.

	es	**ed**	**ing**
1. wave	________	________	________
2. time	________	________	________
3. smile	________	________	________
4. judge	________	________	________
5. cause	________	________	________

DIRECTIONS: Form new words by adding the suffixes **er** and **est**.

	er	**est**
1. safe	________	________
2. grave	________	________
3. wise	________	________
4. large	________	________
5. brave	________	________

DIRECTIONS: Write the root for each of the following words.

coddles	________	delegated	________
receiver	________	excitement	________
nicest	________	blazing	________
gentler	________	cringed	________
leaving	________	latest	________
promised	________	shining	________
stranger	________	crumbled	________

Lesson 128 - Suffixes: Dropping the Final e

Rule: When a word ends in final **e**, drop the **e** before adding a suffix that begins with a vowel.

DIRECTIONS: Add the suffix to the root below the line to complete each sentence. Use your dictionary for the correct spelling if necessary.

1. The hamburgers were ______________________ on the grill at the church picnic.
   sizzle + ing

2. The ______________________ was very silent and prayerful during the consecration.
   congregate + ion

3. The homeschoolers found the racing contests ______________________.
   excite + ing

4. Dad said he would help Mother with ______________________ our schoolwork.
   grade + ing

5. The pope ______________________ at the faithful gathered in St. Peter's Square.
   smile + ed

6. Tom and I ______________________ instead of fighting over the basketball.
   compromise + ed

7. Most ______________________ Infant of Prague, bless our home school!
   adore + able

8. The ______________________ is the most important part of the Mass.
   consecrate + ion

9. They visited their grandmother because they ______________________ about her.
   care + ed

10. It is not ______________________ to be late to Mass without a good reason.
    accept + able

11. The family was praying and ______________________ for a miracle.
    hope + ing

12. The ______________________ learned about Jesus from missionaries.
    trade + ers

Lesson 129 - Suffixes: more than one

DIRECTIONS: Many words have more than one suffix. Read aloud each word in the list below. Underline the first suffix and circle the second suffix. Remember, **s** can be a suffix.

lacerations	carefully	effortlessly	migrations	timelessness
trumpeters	softening	defendants	wonderfully	thoughtlessness
frightening	fearfully	sinfulness	fearfulness	hopelessness
dampened	powerfully	distractions	attendances	consultations

DIRECTIONS: Circle the word(s) in each sentence with more than one suffix. Then write its root on the line.

1. The students were thoughtfully memorizing their catechism. ____________________

   ____
2. Some bystanders moistened a sponge and tried to make Jesus drink from it. ____________________
3. Because of Jeff's carelessness, his bike rusted in the rain. ____________________
4. The shepherds looked adoringly at Baby Jesus. ____________________
5. Joyfully, the congregation sang hymns at Mass. ____________________
6. When Mary first appeared to the children at Fatima, they were frightened. ____________________
7. The Lord blessed Abraham wonderfully. ____________________
8. Hopefully, the new parish hall will be finished soon. ____________________
9. My dad carefully removed the splinter from my hand. ____________________
10. "He that has My commandments, and keeps them, he it is who loves Me." ____________________
11. Approvingly, the Holy Spirit and God the Father looked down on the Baptism of Jesus. ____________________

Lesson 130 - Suffixes: More than one

DIRECTIONS: Read each sentence aloud and circle the words with more than one suffix. Then write each root on the line. Remember, **s** can be a suffix.

1. The thoughtfulness of the volunteers was an inspiration to all those they had helped.

   ____

2. The congregations of all the Catholic churches in the county gathered together for a Christmas celebration. ________________________

3. The chorus sang joyfully at the 11:45 Mass at Our Sorrowful Mother Shrine.

   ____

4. The cheerfulness of the nuns on the hospital staff was contagious.

   ____

5. The parish hall was beautifully decorated in all shades of green for St. Patrick's Day.

   ____

6. Everyone felt heartened at the generosity of the community to the flood victims.

   ____

7. Catholics in different countries have celebrations for different feast days.

   ____

8. The peacefulness of the Irish countryside gave no evidence of the former battleground.

   ____

9. The man's attitude was softened after speaking with the Curé of Ars.

   ____

10. Dr. Morris, a good Catholic doctor, always says a prayer before each of his operations.

    ____

Lesson 131 - Suffixes: Words ending in y

Rule: If a word ends in **y** preceded by a consonant, change the **y** to **i** and add **es** to make the word plural. If a word ends in **y** preceded by a vowel, just add **s** to make the word plural.

Examples: country - countries donkey - donkeys

DIRECTIONS: Write the plural form of each word.

glory	______________	navy	______________
county	______________	monkey	______________
story	______________	joy	______________
injury	______________	jury	______________
play	______________	pony	______________
railway	______________	hobby	______________
cowboy	______________	army	______________

Rule: If a word ends in **y** preceded by a consonant, change the **y** to **i** when any suffix is added, except **ing**. If a word ends in **y** preceded by a vowel, just add the suffix.

Examples: fancy - fancier worry - worrying relay - relayed

DIRECTIONS: Write the root for each word below.

happiest	______________	robberies	______________
holier	______________	satisfies	______________
destroying	______________	handiest	______________
heavier	______________	cries	______________
stays	______________	surgeries	______________
riskier	______________	candies	______________
delayed	______________	pitied	______________
cities	______________	hurrying	______________
juries	______________	deliveries	______________
luckily	______________	tries	______________

Lesson 132 - Suffixes: Words ending in y

Rule: If a word ends in **y** preceded by a consonant, change the **y** to **i** when any suffix is added except **ing**. If a word ends in **y** preceded by a vowel, just add the suffix.

DIRECTIONS: Form a new word by putting each root and suffix together. Write the new word on the line. Review the rules for adding suffixes to words.

dizzy + er ____________________

obey+ ed ____________________

study + ed ____________________

duty + s ____________________

try + ing ____________________

merry + est ____________________

valley + s ____________________

pray + ing ____________________

satisfy + ing ____________________

friendly + er ____________________

beauty + ful ____________________

spy + s ____________________

DIRECTIONS: Circle the words which have a suffix after a root ending in y.

1. Mary hopes that we are praying the Rosary every day.
2. Studying our catechism will help us understand the truths about God.
3. We can earn graces by fulfilling our duties at home.
4. St. Teresa of Avila was not satisfied with an easy life, but strived to sacrifice for Jesus.
5. St. Paul wrote that death has no victories, because God has "given us the victory through Our Lord Jesus Christ."
6. Judith sang praise to God Who delivered the Hebrews from the Assyrian army, who were so numerous that "their horses covered the valleys."
7. Some of the children needed to practice several hours to learn the new melodies.
8. When there was an attempt to imprison or stone Paul and Barnabas, they escaped to other cities and went on preaching the Gospel there.
9. Paul and Barnabas scolded the people for praying to statues, crying, "Men, why do you do these things?"
10. Sister Rose was purifying the needle with alcohol.
11. Do you know all the mysteries of the Rosary?
12. Two Jewish spies, who were concealed by Rahab, were sent to Jericho.

Lesson 133 - Suffix: ly

Rule: **1)** If a word ends in **y** preceded by a consonant, change the **y** to **i** when adding the suffix **ly**.

Examples: busy + ly = busily heavy + ly = heavily merry + ly = merrily
There are a few exceptions, such as **dryly**, **shyly** and **slyly**.

2) When **ly** is added to a word ending in **le**, the **le** is dropped. Otherwise, the word would be difficult to pronounce.

Example: pebble + ly = pebbly

DIRECTIONS: Add **ly** to each word. Refer to the rules above. Write the new word on the line.

possible ____________________	probable ____________________
lucky ____________________	noisy ____________________
hasty ____________________	bubble ____________________
easy ____________________	wrinkle ____________________
crumble ____________________	gloomy ____________________
wiggle ____________________	happy ____________________
simple ____________________	memorable ____________________

DIRECTIONS: Write the root for each underlined word.

1. The girls were reprimanded for being too giggly in religion class.

   ____

2. The altar boys were busily preparing for the baptism. ____________________
3. Catherine was terribly excited that they would be visiting the Vatican.

   ____

4. "We're probably going to confession at 3:30," said Molly. ____________________
5. Mr. Smith lazily strolled home after church. ____________________
6. Luckily, we took the right bus to the March for Life. ____________________
7. The Murphys were doubly blessed with twin babies. ____________________
8. The boys walked hastily to church to get to Mass on time.____________________

Lesson 134 - Suffix: ly

DIRECTIONS: Fifteen words that end in **y** or **le** are hidden in the puzzle below. Some go across, others go up and down. Circle each word as you find it in the puzzle, then add **ly** to each word and write the new word on the lines below.

V	O	L	U	N	T	A	R	Y	H	W	I
P	V	G	R	E	E	D	Y	S	E	O	N
R	B	V	S	O	B	R	T	H	A	R	F
O	S	I	W	E	A	R	Y	A	V	T	A
B	T	S	N	G	W	R	C	B	Y	H	L
A	L	I	W	O	R	D	Y	B	S	Y	L
B	U	B	B	L	E	S	H	Y	P	R	I
L	A	L	W	R	I	N	K	L	E	W	B
E	M	E	W	R	I	G	G	L	E	C	L
X	P	R	E	A	S	O	N	A	B	L	E

Lesson 135 - Suffix Review

DIRECTIONS: Add the suffixes to the roots to form new words. Complete the story on this page by writing the new words on the lines.

Kateri Tekakwitha

The priest had taught me about God the Father, God the Son, and the Great Holy Spirit.

He taught me about the ______________________ Mother and St. Joseph, too. Then came
Bless + ed

the day to be ______________________ in 1676 on Easter Sunday. They gave me the name
baptize + ed

of Kateri or Katherine. My heart sang out for the joy of it. The Holy Spirit, ______________________
enter + ing

into me at Baptism, was to raise me in four years to a high degree of ______________________ .
holy + ness

God kept me for two years in the Indian lodge to triumph over the unbelief of the Iroquois, to serve

as an example for the new Church of the ______________________, and to increase my merit by
Mohawk + s

many ______________________.
trial + s

After my death, a Jesuit Father at the Mission of the Sault, wrote that he had ______________________
close + ly

______________________ my conduct after Baptism to see if I ______________________ out
watch + ed carry +ed

his ______________________. He ______________________ that after ______________________
direct + ion + s declare + ed care + ful

______________________, he had not ______________________ one point in
examine + ation notice + ed

which I had ______________________ since I had become a Christian. I had to do this in
relax + ed

______________________ that were very much against ______________________ my
surround + ing + s live + ing

______________________ ______________________.
baptism + al vow + s

One of the great ______________________, ______________________ among the
demon + s especial + ly

______________________, ______________________ to rob the gift of grace in my soul, was
savage + s strive + ing

that of impurity. I was always ______________________ to flee any occasion of impurity, and so I had
care + ful

no trouble in ______________________ it. God, of course, gave me very special ______________________
avoid + ing grace + s

while ______________________ in such ______________________. God always
live + ing surround + ing + s

______________________ ______________________ grace to avoid every sin if we ask for
give + s suffice + ient

and accept God's grace.

Lesson 136 - Review

DIRECTIONS: Read the following words aloud.

washing	referring	praying	saddest
dinner	parted	sleeping	swimming
knitting	canning	fattest	letter
equipment	padded	relentless	manned
quickly	waved	waving	smiling
caused	safer	gravest	wiser
largest	delegated	blazing	excitement
cringed	shining	crumbled	grading
acceptable	hoping	traders	congregation
carefully	fearfulness	joyfully	thoughtlessness
wonderfully	powerfully	sinfulness	dampened
attendance	heartened	holier	cheerfulness
destroying	heavier	delayed	peacefulness
juries	cries	heartiest	pitied
studying	fulfilling	duties	countries
valleys	crying	spies	satisfied
possibly	luckily	hastily	easily
simply	probably	noisily	bubbly
happily	hopefully	cried	memorably

Lesson 137 - Plurals for Words Ending in f, fe, & ff

Rule: If a word ends in **f** or **fe**, the **f** or **fe** is usually changed to **v,** and **es** is added to make the word plural. **Example:** leaf - leaves

Chief, **belief**, **reef**, and **roof** are four exceptions.
Any word that ends in double **f** (**ff**) is made plural by adding **s**. **Example:** cuffs

DIRECTIONS: Write the plural form of each underlined word in the space provided.

1. My mother keeps a statue of the Blessed Mother on a shelf. ____________________
2. Being a wife is a very important vocation. ____________________
3. The Immaculate Conception is a belief of the Catholic Church. ____________________
4. Father O'Connor put on a scarf to walk from the church to the rectory. ____________________
5. Moses carried his staff with him on the journey to the Promised Land. ____________________
6. St. Martin de Porres lived his life for the greater glory of God. ____________________
7. Moses became angry when the people worshipped a golden calf. ____________________
8. Two men were crucified with Jesus, but only one thief repented. ____________________
9. Mother asked Jimmy to buy a loaf of bread. ____________________
10. Father Constantine purchased a fantastic icon of the Flight to Egypt, done with gold leaf. ____________________
11. King Herod told the girl, "I will give you whatever you ask, even if it is half of my kingdom." ____________________
12. Abraham had raised his knife to kill his son when the angel stopped him. ____________________
13. When the chief steward had tasted the wine, he asked why the good wine was served later. ____________________
14. When the prophet Isaias predicted the Kingdom of Christ, he said the "wolf shall dwell with the lamb." ____________________
15. St. Mark wrote that "to love one's neighbor as one's self" is a greater thing than sacrifice. ____________________

Lesson 138 - Plurals for Words Ending in f, fe, & ff

Rule: If a word ends in **f** or **fe**, the **f** or **fe** is usually changed to **v**, and **es** is added to make the word plural. **Chief, belief, reef,** and **roof** are four exceptions.

Any word that ends in double **f** (**ff**) is made plural by adding **s**.

DIRECTIONS: Write the plural form for the nouns below. Check in the dictionary.

knife ____________________ pontiff ____________________

beef ____________________ turf ____________________

cliff ____________________ puff ____________________

ourself ____________________ proof ____________________

bluff ____________________ roof ____________________

wife ____________________ life ____________________

chef ____________________ brief ____________________

hoof ____________________ sheaf ____________________

DIRECTIONS: Using at least five of the plural words above, write five sentences on the lines below.

1. ____

____

2. ____

____

3. ____

____

4. ____

____

5. ____

____

Lesson 139 - Plural Form for Words Ending in o

Rule: If a word ends in **o**, usually **s** is added to make the word plural.
Examples: radios, pianos

Some exceptions are made plural by adding **es**.
Examples of Exceptions: hero - heroes   potato - potatoes   tomato - tomatoes

DIRECTIONS: Complete each sentence by writing the plural form of the word at the right. Use the dictionary as you wish.

1. Angels and saints are often pictured with ________________ over their heads. halo
2. We must be careful to watch only wholesome ________________ which support our values and morals. video
3. The saints are ________________ to be respected and imitated. hero
4. The presidential ________________ opposed good pro-life legislation. veto
5. James carries two ________________ of the pope in his wallet. photo
6. Mrs. O'Brien brought ________________ to the church picnic. tangelo
7. Catherine was learning all about ________________ from her father. ratio
8. Jane and Maria are growing ________________ as part of their science project. tomato
9. John and Brian are both ________________ in the church choir. alto
10. The Davis children learned all about ________________ as part of their music class. piano
11. The Mexicans wear ________________ to keep the sun out of their eyes. sombrero
12. There has been an increase in the number of ________________ in our country. tornado
13. Grandpa has two ________________ outside his home. patio
14. Our ________________ have only AM stations. radio
15. I love to attend the ________________ in Wyoming. rodeo

Lesson 140 - Plural Form for Words Ending in o

DIRECTIONS: Fifteen words ending in **o** are hidden in the puzzle below. Some go across, and others go up and down. Circle each word as you find it in the puzzle. Then write the plural form of the words on the lines provided.

F	R	O	P	M	P	K	A	V	C	O	P
M	P	H	A	L	O	S	T	E	F	P	O
E	U	O	T	D	C	T	O	T	H	S	R
M	E	B	I	R	S	U	S	O	E	I	T
E	B	O	O	P	H	D	G	K	R	L	F
N	L	M	Y	I	V	I	D	E	O	O	O
T	O	R	N	A	D	O	Y	F	S	W	L
O	H	T	S	T	E	M	P	O	R	O	I
G	B	C	F	E	H	S	T	E	R	E	O
I	N	F	E	R	N	O	L	R	W	B	Y

________________ ________________ ________________

________________ ________________ ________________

________________ ________________ ________________

________________ ________________ ________________

________________ ________________ ________________

Lesson 141 - Plural Forms

Rule: Some words do not change at all in their plural form.

DIRECTIONS: The words in the exercise below are the same in their singular and plural forms. If the word names a food that comes from a plant, write *P*. If it names an animal or fish, or food that comes from an animal or fish, write *A*.

1. _____ yogurt	_____ kale	_____ cocoa	_____ sheep
2. _____ coffee	_____ cauliflower	_____ spinach	_____ salsa
3. _____ cattle	_____ pork	_____ moose	_____ milk
4. _____ cereal	_____ ketchup	_____ tuna	_____ corn
5. _____ lettuce	_____ garlic	_____ mustard	_____ popcorn
6. _____ deer	_____ coleslaw	_____ oatmeal	_____ fish

Rule: Some words change completely in their plural form.

DIRECTIONS: Look in the dictionary and write the plural forms of the words below.

goose ____________________	tooth ____________________
man ____________________	foot ____________________
mouse____________________	ox ____________________
child ____________________	woman ____________________

DIRECTIONS: Here are some other plural forms which may not be familiar to you. Write the correct word next to each definition.

singular	**plural**	**singular**	**plural**
alumnus	alumni	fungus	fungi
nebula	nebulas	crisis	crises
oasis	oases	formula	formulas

1. ____________________ in the desert fertile places with water
2. ____________________ former students of a certain school or college
3. ____________________ a milk mixture for feeding a baby

Lesson 142 - Plural Forms

DIRECTIONS: Match the words on the left to the definitions on the right.

1. mice	______	a. ground or rolled oats, cooked as porridge
2. fish	______	b. what you use for biting and chewing
3. nebulae	______	c. small rodents found in houses and fields
4. coffee	______	d. largest animal of the deer family
5. moose	______	e. powder made from roasted cacao
6. women	______	f. cold-blooded animal with fins and gills
7. spinach	______	g. thick, semisolid food often flavored with fruit
8. milk	______	h. a favorite morning drink for adults
9. tuna	______	i. a favorite drink of children to have with cookies
10. geese	______	j. fertile places with water in the desert
11. oatmeal	______	k. cabbage with spreading, curled leaves
12. kale	______	l. more than one adult female
13. yogurt	______	m. good for making sandwiches on Friday
14. garlic	______	n. strong-smelling plant bulb, used to season
15. ketchup	______	o. cloudlike patches seen in the night sky
16. teeth	______	p. plant with dark-green, edible leaves; Popeye's favorite food
17. cocoa	______	q. long-necked water birds
18. oases	______	r. thick sauce of tomatoes

Lesson 143 - Syllables

Rule: **1)** Double vowels stand for only one vowel sound. (r**ea**d, sp**oo**n)
2) A prefix or suffix is a syllable in itself if it contains a vowel sound. (**pre**serve, old**er**)
3) Some prefixes and suffixes have more than one syllable. (**super**visor)

DIRECTIONS: Read each word. Then write the number of vowels you see, the number of vowel sounds you hear, and the number of syllables in each word.

	Vowels Seen	**Vowel Sounds**	**Syllables**
congregation	______	______	______
adventurer	______	______	______
ecclesiastical	______	______	______
illuminate	______	______	______
Benediction	______	______	______
indivisible	______	______	______
biographical	______	______	______
archangels	______	______	______
imprimatur	______	______	______
disciple	______	______	______
Transfiguration	______	______	______
priesthood	______	______	______
prepared	______	______	______
supervisor	______	______	______
righteous	______	______	______
godchild	______	______	______
delegation	______	______	______
fatherhood	______	______	______
angelic	______	______	______
gentleman	______	______	______
Christianity	______	______	______
Confirmation	______	______	______

Lesson 144 - Syllables

DIRECTIONS: See if you can find fourteen words in the puzzle below. Work from left to right and then top to bottom. Circle the words as you find them. Write them on the lines. Then divide them into syllables using vertical lines.

S	C	R	I	P	T	U	R	E	C	M	S
H	O	L	Y	A	M	S	E	R	H	D	E
F	L	B	C	S	G	O	S	P	E	L	M
P	A	P	A	C	Y	B	P	N	R	E	I
R	B	H	X	H	D	E	E	O	U	R	N
E	T	O	N	A	G	D	C	F	B	H	A
P	L	M	P	L	O	I	T	S	U	P	R
A	W	I	O	F	F	E	R	T	O	R	Y
R	G	L	W	G	E	N	E	S	I	S	V
E	D	Y	B	I	R	T	H	D	A	Y	A

_______________ _______________

_______________ _______________

_______________ _______________

_______________ _______________

_______________ _______________

_______________ _______________

_______________ _______________

Lesson 145 - Syllables

Compound words are made up of two or more words.

Rule: Divide a compound word between the smaller words that make the compound word.
Examples: God|child fire|man church|bell

DIRECTIONS: Underline the compound words in the sentences. Then divide them into syllables by drawing vertical lines.

---

1. Our church is decorated with many red poinsettias on Christmas Day, which is Jesus' birthday.
2. Men who are entering the priesthood try to be Christlike in their thoughts and actions.
3. The annual Byzantine potluck dinner was held downstairs in the church basement.
4. The O'Briens give part of their paycheck to Human Life International every month.
5. The fireworks will begin at nightfall at the St. Cyril church picnic.
6. The bridesmaids and bridegroom were at the Church of the Epiphany before the bride.

Rule: When a word ends in **le** preceded by a consonant, divide the word before that consonant.
Example: sam|ple ram|ble tan|gle

DIRECTIONS: Divide these words into syllables using vertical lines.

---

disciple	apostle	honorable	gentle	ample
bearable	double	memorable	wiggle	crumble
tingle	giggle	acceptable	jingle	assemble
audible	terrible	adorable	jiggle	humble
flexible	paddle	infallible	coddle	capable

Lesson 146 - Syllables

DIRECTIONS: On the first line after each word, write the number of syllables in the word. On the second line, divide the word into syllables using vertical lines.

archdiocese _____ ____________________

backache _____ ____________________

knowledgeable _____ ____________________

sacrifice _____ ____________________

American _____ ____________________

cherubim _____ ____________________

conservative _____ ____________________

Epiphany _____ ____________________

billfold _____ ____________________

Genesis _____ ____________________

parishioner _____ ____________________

overseas _____ ____________________

Scripture _____ ____________________

president _____ ____________________

respect _____ ____________________

seminary _____ ____________________

papacy _____ ____________________

archangel _____ ____________________

Fatima _____ ____________________

Lourdes _____ ____________________

angelic _____ ____________________

Trinity _____ ____________________

Lesson 147 - Plurals

DIRECTIONS: Read the paragraphs aloud. Complete each unfinished sentence by writing the plural form of each word on the line above it.

The saints are ______________ (hero) whose ______________ (life) we should all try to imitate. Some of the saints had ______________ (motto) such as, "Death before sin." All of the saints had virtues which all ______________ (man), ______________ (woman) and ______________ (child) should strive to attain. For example, we could each try to be more humble, kind, and holy.

Many saints were killed because of their ______________ (belief) and their refusal to deny those ______________ (belief). Many holy ______________ (man) and ______________ (woman) gladly gave their ______________ (life) or suffered greatly for Jesus. We should ask ______________ (ourself) if we are willing to suffer, even a little, for Christ. Let us hope the answer is "Yes," and that we, too, will someday be saints in Heaven.

The three shepherd ______________ (child) of Fatima, although they were very young, practiced many ______________ (sacrifice) for poor ______________ (sinner). They had seen ______________ (soul) falling into hell as many as ______________ (snowflake) falling from the sky.

Lesson 148 - Phonics Practice

DIRECTIONS: Read the paragraphs aloud.

A. The Irish people are famous for their friendliness, their easy smiles, and their humor. Many Irish families still farm their land and raise sheep or dairy cows. They also make many things by hand, like beautiful glass bowls and cups, hand-knit sweaters, and white linen cloth. In some parts of Ireland, you can still see the old stone and clay cottages with their straw-thatched roofs. The larger cities, like Dublin (the capital), Limerick, and Waterford, have modern buildings and industry.

Family life is very strong in Ireland. Often parents and children will gather with their neighbors for celebrations. They sing Irish songs and dance the special Irish dance called the "Irish Jig" (from: Our Friends From Other Lands, pp. 14-15).

B. And it came to pass on a certain day, as He sat teaching, that there were also Pharisees and doctors of the law sitting by, that were come out of every town of Galilee, and Judea and Jerusalem; and the power of the Lord was to heal them. And behold, men brought in a bed a man who had the palsy: and they sought means to bring him in, and to lay him before Him. And when they could not find by what way they might bring him in, because of the multitude, they went up upon the roof, and let him down through the tiles with his bed into the midst before Jesus. Whose faith when He saw, He said: "Man, thy sins are forgiven thee." And the scribes and Pharisees began to think, saying: "Who is this who speaketh blasphemies? Who can forgive sins, but God alone?" And when Jesus knew their thoughts, answering, He said to them: "What is it you think in your hearts? Which is easier to say, Thy sins are forgiven thee; or to say, Arise and walk? But that you may know that the Son of Man hath power on earth to forgive sins, (He said to the sick of the palsy,) I say to thee, Arise, take up thy bed, and go into thy house." And immediately rising up before them, he took up the bed on which he lay; and he went away to his own house, glorifying God. And all were astonished; and they glorified God. And they were filled with fear, saying: "We have seen wonderful things today" (Luke 5: 17-26).

Lesson 149 - Alphabetizing

Rule: Words are arranged in alphabetical order in a dictionary. When words begin with the same letter or letters, look at the second or next letter to put the words in alphabetical order.

DIRECTIONS: Number the words in each column to show the alphabetical order. Remember to look at the second letter of each word.

priest	______	sacrifice	______	apostles	______
pope	______	shepherd	______	angelic	______
pharisee	______	scrupulous	______	archbishop	______
penitent	______	suffer	______	American	______
paschal	______	seminary	______	Ascension	______

DIRECTIONS: Number the words in these columns to show the alphabetical order. Look at the third letter of each word.

Communion	______	lamb	______	sanctity	______
covenant	______	laity	______	saint	______
cornerstone	______	law	______	salvation	______
congregation	______	Latin	______	sacrament	______
courteous	______	layman	______	satisfaction	______

DIRECTIONS: Unscramble each sentence by writing the words in alphabetical order. Look at the second or third letters when words begin with the same letters.

1. her confessed Abigail sins

   ____

2. Jesus to everyone was preached well-advised

   ____

3. spirits angels pure are

   ____

Lesson 150 - Dictionary: Guide Words

Rule: The **guide words** at the top of a dictionary page help you to find entries quickly. The guide word on the left tells you the first entry word on the page. The guide word on the right tells you the last entry word on the page. The other entries on the page are between those two words in alphabetical order.

DIRECTIONS: Write the number of the guide words that would be on the same dictionary page next to each entry word below.

1. angel / anger ______ heroic
2. hermit / holy ______ Beatitudes
3. prophesy / proverbs ______ prophets
4. beatific / Benedictines ______ disciple
5. diocese / discipline ______ Angelus

1. candle / canonization ______ cathedral
2. cardinal / cassock ______ cemetery
3. catechetics / Catholic ______ canon
4. celebrant / ceremony ______ character
5. chant / charity ______ Carmelite

DIRECTIONS: Read the guide words at the top of each column. Circle the one word in the column that would **not** be on the same dictionary page as those guide words.

1. **abbess / alleluia**
   absolution
   action
   age
   alms
   Adam

2. **habit / hermit**
   halo
   heaven
   heresy
   heroic
   harmony

3. **papacy / Passover**
   parish
   pastor
   paradise
   parable
   paschal

4. **decade / demon**
   dedication
   decree
   delegation
   deontology
   degree

5. **sin / spiritual**
   sponsor
   sister
   soul
   solemn
   society

6. **Madonna / marriage**
   Mariology
   Magnificat
   martyr
   marks
   Magisterium

Lesson 151 - Dictionary: Pronunciation Key

Rule: The respelling that follows a dictionary entry shows how to pronounce that word. Use the dictionary's pronunciation key to help you pronounce each respelling.

DIRECTIONS: Look at the full pronunciation key.

a	p**a**t	k	**k**ick, **c**all	th	**th**in
a	p**ay**	l	**l**id	*th*	**th**is
ar	c**ar**e	m	**m**u**m**	u	c**u**t
a	f**a**ther	n	**n**o, sudde**n**	ur	**ur**ge, t**er**m, f**ir**m, w**or**d h**ear**d
b	**b**i**b**	ng	thi**ng**	v	**v**al**v**e
ch	**ch**ur**ch**	o	p**o**t, h**o**rrid	w	**w**ith
d	**d**ee**d**	o	t**oe**, h**oa**rse	y	**y**es
e	p**e**t	o	c**au**ght, p**aw**	yoo	ab**u**se, **u**se
e	b**ee**	oi	n**oi**se	z	**z**ebra, **x**ylem
f	**f**i**f**e, **ph**ase	oo	t**oo**k	zh	vi**s**ion
g	**g**a**g**	oo	b**oo**t	ə	represents: **a**bout, it**e**m edi**b**le, gall**o**p circ**u**s
h	**h**at	ou	**ou**t	r	butt**er**
hw	**wh**ich	p	**p**o**p**		
i	p**i**t	r	**r**oa**r**		
i	p**ie**, b**y**	s	**s**au**c**e		
ir	p**ier**	sh	**sh**ip, di**sh**		
j	**j**u**dg**e, **g**em	t	**t**igh**t**, stopp**ed**		

Rule: When a word has two or more syllables, one syllable is stressed, or accented more than any other. In the dictionary, an **accent mark** (´) shows the syllable that is said with more stress.

DIRECTIONS: Use the pronunciation key above and accent marks to say each respelling below. Then circle the word that goes with that respelling.

1. rel´ik — relic — relief — relax
2. pri-par´ — preserve — prepare — prepay
3. gras´roots´ — grassland — grasping — grassroots
4. ej´ə-kat — edition — educate — education
5. ser´ə-fim — seraphim — serape — serenade
6. mar´tər — martial — marvel — martyr
7. kre-a´tər — creature — Creator — creative
8. an´jəl — angle — anger — angel
9. dis´ə-plin — disciple — discipline — discard
10. hom´ə-le — homily — homey — humble

Lesson 152 - Dictionary: Entries

Rule: Entry words are often found in the dictionary without suffixes such as **s**, **es**, **ed**, or **ing**. When you search for a word in the dictionary, look for the word without those suffixes.

DIRECTIONS: Match each word in dark print with the entry word you would look for in the dictionary. Write the number of the correct word on the line in front of its entry word.

1. **shrines**	_____ a. kneel		6. **believed**	_____ f. angel
2. **praying**	_____ b. separate		7. **shipping**	_____ g. sisters
3. **separating**	_____ c. pray		8. **sister**	_____ h. sacrament
4. **spotted**	_____ d. shrine		9. **angels**	_____ i. ship
5. **kneeling**	_____ e. spot		10. **sacraments**	_____ j. believe

DIRECTIONS: Read the paragraph below. Notice the underlined words. On the lines below the paragraph, write each word as you find it as a dictionary entry word.

As the sun rose one morning, a little girl named Jacinta skipped through the gate to the sheepyard. Jacinta was seven years old and not much taller than the sheep she watched each day. She had a name for each one of them, and loved to give them little snacks (from Our Friends From Other Lands, p.96).

1. ______________________
2. ______________________
3. ______________________
4. ______________________
5. ______________________
6. ______________________
7. ______________________

Lesson 153 - Dictionary: Word Meanings

Rule: Sometimes you may notice in a dictionary entry that a word has a small raised number to the right of it. This tells you that there is another word pronounced and spelled the same way, but has a completely different meaning or origin.

DIRECTIONS: Read these entries. Then decide which word to use to complete each sentence below. Write the entry word and **n.** (for noun) or **v.** (for verb) on the line in each sentence.

stick n. small branch broken or cut off
stick v. pierce; attach as by pinning or gluing

hail n. frozen raindrops
hail v. cheer, shout to

cell n. small room as in a prison
cell n. device for generating electricity chemically

stoop v. bend the body forward
stoop n. small porch

order n. monastic or fraternal brotherhood
order v. command, request

1. Father Anselmo came to America from Italy as a priest in the Cistercian ________________________ of monks.

2. Peter was placed in a ________________________, but escaped when an angel opened the gate for him.

3. When Jesus was hanging on the cross, someone told a guard to ________________________ Him in the side with a spear.

4. Our neighbors have a statue of Mary displayed on their ________________________ in front of their house.

5. We stood in the church foyer for ten minutes one day because we did not want to go out in the ________________________.

Lesson 154 - Dictionary: Word Meanings

Rule: When there is more than one meaning for an entry word, the different meanings are numbered. The most commonly used meaning is usually listed first.

DIRECTIONS: Read these dictionary entries. Then decide which meaning of a word is used in each sentence below. Write the correct word and its definition number on the line in each sentence.

harmony n.
1. pleasing agreement of parts
2. agreement in ideas, action, etc.
3. pleasing combination of musical tones

age n.
1. length of time of existence
2. time of getting full legal rights
3. historical period

remain v.
1. be left when part is gone
2. stay
3. continue

truth n.
1. being true, honest
2. that which is true
3. established fact

1. Before Adam and Eve fell from grace, they lived in ______________________ with everything around them.
2. As Pinocchio learned, we must always tell the ______________________ because "a lie keeps growing until it's as plain as the nose on your face."
3. Noah's ____________________ was quite remarkable, as he lived to be 950 years old.
4. During his annual retreat, Father Dominic said he would ______________________ after Mass to hear confessions.

Lesson 155 - Dictionary

DIRECTIONS: Read these entries. Then follow the instructions below.

float(flot) v. -ing	1. to be or cause to be suspended within or on the surface of a fluid 2. to drift randomly from place to place
bundle(bun´dl) n.	1. a group of things fastened together 2. slang. a large amount of money
reed(red) n.	1. any of several tall swamp or marsh grasses with jointed hollow stalks 2. a primitive wind instrument made with a hollow reed stalk
llama(la´m) n.	a South American ruminant, *Lama pervana*, related to the camel and raised for its soft, fleecy wool
wool(wool) n.	1. the soft, thick, often curly hair of some mammals, especially sheep
people(pe´pəl) n.	1. human beings 2. the body of persons living under one government in the same country
holy(ho´ le) adj.	1. belonging to, derived from, or associated with a divine power: sacred 2. regarded with or deserving of worship or veneration: revered 3. spiritually perfect: saintly

1. Circle each word that would come before the word **holy** if in alphabetical order.

   hole honest honor hope

   homily hold homage holly

2. Circle the guide words that would be on the same page as the word **people**.

   penny/perceive pectin/pelage pergola/permanent

3. Write each word having only one syllable from the entries at the top.

   ______________________ ______________________ ______________________

4. Write each entry word whose first syllable is the stressed syllable.

   __________________ __________________ __________________ __________________

5. Complete the following sentence with one of the entry words from above. Write the correct word and the definition number on the line.

   St. Martin de Porres was a very ______________________ man who did much to help the poor.

DIRECTIONS: Write the number of the meaning of the word in dark print that is used in each sentence below.

_____ 1. Some **people** are very honest and trustworthy.

_____ 2. The boat from which Jesus was preaching was **floating** on the Sea of Galilee.

_____ 3. Our Catholic church is a very **holy** and sacred place.

Definitions and Rules

The **vowels** are **a, e, i, o, u,** and sometimes **y** and **w**.

The **consonants** are the remaining letters and usually **y** and **w**.

A **consonant blend** consists of two or more consonants sounded together in such a way that each is heard—**bl**ock, **tr**ust, **cr**ab, **sw**am.

A **consonant digraph** consists of two consonants that together represent one sound—**wh**im, **th**ick, **th**en, **ch**ur**ch**, **sh**ower, ba**ck**.

Short-Vowel Rule: If a word or syllable has only one vowel and it comes at the beginning or between two consonants, the vowel usually stands for a short sound—**at, it, sag, fox**.

Long Vowel Rule I: If a one-part word or syllable has two vowels, the first vowel usually stands for a long sound and the second is silent—**pain, kite, came, sheep**.

Long Vowel Rule II: If a word or syllable has one vowel and it comes at the end of the word or syllable, the vowel usually stands for a long sound—**me, pony, go, stupid**.

Y As a Vowel Rule:

1) If **y** is the only "vowel" at the end of a one-syllable word, **y** has the sound of long **i—cry, my, try**.

2) If **y** is the only vowel at the end of a word of more than one syllable, **y** usually has a sound almost like long **e—glory, navy**.

A **vowel digraph** is a double vowel that does not follow Long-Vowel Rule I—sch**oo**l, c**oo**k, spr**ea**d, **au**tomatic, l**aw**n, **ei**ght.

A **diphthong** consists of two vowels blended together to form a sound—cl**ou**d, n**ew**, t**oi**l.

Soft C and G rule: When **c** or **g** is followed by **e, i** or **y**, it usually stands for a soft sound—**nice, city, gym, change**.

To make a noun show **possession**:

1) Add **'s** to a singular noun.

cat's **John's** **mother's**

2) Just add an **'** to a plural noun ending in **s**.

girls' **Smiths'** **kittens'**

3) Add **'s** to a plural noun not ending in **s**.

oxen's **men's** **mice's**

A **root** is a word or a word part from which other words can be made.

pos **duct** **spec**

A **suffix** is a word part added to the end of a root.

bak**er** help**ful** kind**ness**

A **prefix** is a word part that is added in front of a root.

prolife **in**valid **un**happy

A **compound word** is made up of two or more other words.

notebook **cupcake** **bluebird**

To make a word mean more than one:

1) Usually add **s**.

boys **girls** **toys**

2) If a word ends in **x, z, ss, sh,** or **ch,** usually add **es.**

foxes **churches** **masses**

3) If a word ends in **y** preceded by a consonant, change the **y** to **i** and add **es**.

glories **counties** **flurries**

4) If a word ends in **f** or **fe**, usually change the **f** or **fe** to **v** and add **es**.

thieves **shelves** **knives**

5) If a word ends in **o**, usually just add **s** to make the word plural. Some exceptions are made plural by adding **es**.

hero-heroes **halo-halos** **tomato-tomatoes**

6) Some words change their vowel sound in the plural form.

woman-women **goose-geese** **foot-feet**

To add other suffixes:

1) When a short-vowel word ends in a single consonant, usually double the consonant before adding a suffix that begins with a vowel.

swimming **stunned** **splatter**

2) When a word ends in silent **e**, drop the **e** before adding a suffix that begins with a vowel.

making **smiled** **wisest**

3) When a word ends in **y** preceded by a consonant, change the **y** to **i** before adding a suffix other than **ing**.

holier **signifies** **merriest**

Syllabication Rules:

When a single consonant comes between two vowels in a word, the word is usually divided after the consonant if the first vowel is short.

shiv/er **ped/al**

When a single consonant comes between two vowels in a word, the word is usually divided before the consonant if the first vowel is long.

cu/bic **si/lent**

A word has as many syllables as it has vowel sounds.

A **prefix** is a syllable in itself if it contains a vowel sound. Divide the word between the prefix and the root word. Some prefixes have more than one syllable.

un/certain **dis/connect**

When you divide a compound word into syllables:

1) Divide the compound word between the words that make it up.

2) Second, if necessary, divide the smaller words into syllables.

When a word ends in **le** preceded by a consonant, divide the word before that consonant.

cas/tle **peb/ble**

NOTES

NOTES